The Hungry Manager

By Desiree Cox

The Hungry Manager

Published by Praeceptor Consulting

Copyright 2012 Desiree Cox

First published 2013

ISBN-13: 978-1482776362

ISBN-10: 1482776367

Acknowledgements

People come on training programmes with the primary expectation of developing their knowledge or skill in particular areas, yet seldom realising how much they give in return. I would like to thank all the delegates who have attended my workshops and courses for helping me to develop my own knowledge through answering their questions, considering their problems, marking their assignments and sharing their experiences. There are too many to name; however, each learner has taught me something and I thank each one.

My thanks also go to my colleagues and associates for selflessly sharing their knowledge with me. In particular, my appreciation to Oliver Tate, Allan Miller, Vic Hartley, Jane Fish, Keith Holdaway and Jim McDermott.

Once again, I would like to thank Caroline Wren for volunteering to edit this book for me and for proof-reading it so promptly and efficiently.

When you work from home, it invariably spills into family life and I am so fortunate in the amazing support I receive from my husband and daughters – thank you.

Table of Contents

Introduction

Congratulations – you have taken the first step in finding out more about management and leadership. This may be because you have been newly promoted to the role or simply because you now want to develop your knowledge and skills further. 'The Hungry Manager' is aimed at people wanting to know more about management and leadership, hungry to learn.

This book examines the roles of managers and leaders, considering the varying responsibilities, together with the knowledge and skills required, to fulfil the requirements.

It introduces a fresh concept – the Management Wheel – and offers you the opportunity to enhance your own self-awareness through discovering where your strengths and your improvement areas as a manager lie and the impact this may have on those around you and your organisation. Once you have taken the Management Wheel test, you may choose to focus on certain areas of this book or you may prefer to work through the book in order.

We will explore the theories and concepts of management, together with examples where these work in practice. Each chapter will offer you opportunities to reflect on your own practice, providing food for thought for **YOU** in **YOUR** role. Look out for the 'Learning Bites' in every chapter which give you activities to consider.

Enjoy the learning journey!

Desirée Cox

Management versus Leadership

Managers and leaders in organisation have a dominant role to play in the success or failure of an organisation. However, how do we differentiate between the role of the 'manager' versus the role of the 'leader'? This is a question that baffles many and has no confirmed answer.

The Business Dictionary offers the following definition of a manager[i]:

> 'An individual who is in charge of a certain group of tasks, or a certain subset of a company. A manager often has a staff of people who report to him or her'

This can be broken down into different types of manager – staff manager, project manager, first line manager.

For a leader, the Business Dictionary provides this definition[ii]:

> 'A person or thing that holds a dominant or superior position within its field, and is able to exercise a high degree of control or influence over others'

So is there much difference between the roles of manager and leader? Or does it depend on the organisation or the people you talk to?

Learning Bite:
How would you define the roles of a manager and a leader? Where do you see differences and/or similarities?

Most will agree that leadership has undergone fundamental changes over the past century veering from a very autocratic style to a much more democratic style where more power is given to other people in the organisation. Before we explore the modern meanings of management and leadership, let's look at history to find out more about how management and leadership have evolved.

History of Management and Leadership

Whilst we could go back to the days of the Roman Empire for a lesson on leadership, we will begin by looking at the history of management over the past century. There are five established 'schools of management'. Some are well known, others lesser so. These are:

- **Classical School** – from 1880s to 1920s covered scientific management, administrative management and bureaucratic management

- **Behavioural School** – 1930s (briefly) and 1950s looked at human relations and behavioural science

- **Quantitative School** -1940s, then 1960s to 1970s saw a return to the science of management and application of statistical and mathematical theory

- **Systems School** – 1950s looked at management as a system that focused on transformation of inputs into results taking account of the environmental factors

- **Contingency School** – 1960s considered application of management principles influenced by situational factors

We will start by looking at the work of Frederick Taylor (1856-1915), an industrial engineer, who used four principles to revolutionise the manufacturing industry in the USA.

At the beginning of the 20th century, Taylor developed a 'science' of management by introducing a concept to maximise productivity and increase efficiency by minimising workers' skills. He believed that every task, job or role could be broken down into a number of small parts which could easily be timed and taught. He used time and motion studies to optimise job performance, to revolutionise roles and work-stations with the focus on profit and performance. In this way, managers were able to supervise staff more thoroughly and determine pay according to output or results. This management style became known as Taylorism. Although resulting in good performance, it required a lot of management time for supervision of staff and tasks to ensure everything ran smoothly and according to plan.

Strongly criticised for the demeaning effect and demotivating impact on staff, it led to great success in the US manufacturing industry and unprecedented work output during the Second World War.

So Taylorism was an early form of autocratic leadership. Elements of Taylorism will still be seen in some industries and organisations today. However, it is largely acknowledged that such extreme autocracy only serves to demotivate staff and therefore is not necessarily productive in the longer term.

Learning Bite:
Taylorism still works in some areas of industry. Are there areas of your organisation where this could be effective? In what ways could this theory be efficient?

As the century progressed into the 1920s, the focus of management turned to a more bureaucratic style. Organisations became more hierarchical with organisational culture becoming more formal with rules, processes and organisational structures. Organisations became less personal, they became larger and staff were largely recruited based on qualifications and ability, rather than personality.

This bureaucratic style was introduced by the German political economist and sociologist, Max Weber, who claimed that bureaucracy was the ideal way to organise public sector offices. His philosophy spread to the private sector and was based upon the principles of hierarchic levels of control, formal rules and decision making at the higher levels of the organisation to be implemented by the lower levels. It was believed that all staff and customers should be treated equally without consideration for individual differences and staff would be recruited to their posts based on their qualifications.

There is still much evidence of a bureaucratic style in organisations today, particularly in the public sector. Whilst there are both positive and negative aspects to bureaucracy, it remains the most popular way of organising very large companies.

Learning Bite:
Can you identify organisations where there is evidence of a
bureaucratic style of management? What are the signs? Is this
appropriate for this type of organisation?

The 1940s saw a change from scientific management to
administrative management. This theory had been developed by
Henri Fayol and his colleagues who published their work around
the same time as Frederick Taylor, but it was not until the 1940s
that administrative management became more popular. Fayol
categorised the role of a manager into five different functions,
which we would still acknowledge as the core aspects of the
manager role today. These were[iii]:

- To forecast and to plan

- To organise

- To coordinate

- To control

- To command

In addition, he recognised 14 principles of management around
the division of work, the manager's authority and the treatment of
staff.

Learning Bite:
Look back at the first activity you completed. How does your list
compare with the core aspects identified by Henri Fayol?

The 1950s and 1960s saw many further changes and many
management theorists became focused on the 'behavioural'
science of management and human relations – for example,
Abraham Maslow, Douglas McGregor, Elton Mayo and Frederick
Herzberg. We will look at some of these later when we consider
motivation.

The behavioural science of management began to look at human aspects of management and working. They focused on workers' attitudes and the manager's attitude towards them. The Hawthorne Experiments[iv] conducted in the second half of the 1920s by Elton Mayo (1880-1949), an Australian psychologist and sociologist, and his colleagues, concluded that the attitudes of staff and workers are associated with the level of productivity and that the workplace itself is a social system where there are human informal influences on groups and individuals. The initial experiments focused on the effect of light and gave rise to the term 'the Hawthorne effect', which was extended to consider all aspects of the workplace and its effect on staff motivation and, in turn, their productivity, which increased temporarily when changes (usually positive) were made to the environment.

Learning Bite:
How can you relate the Hawthorne effect to your workplace? Can you identify changes or incidents which have triggered increased productivity and how long this impact lasted?

The 1950s also saw the appearance of the systems school and the contingency school. The systems school was developed largely by the biologist, Ludwig von Bertalanffy, and focused on understanding the organisation as a system which considered the transformation between input and output. Its impact was primarily seen on the influence on management in understanding the relationships between different parts of an organisation and external environment. It has been criticized as being complex and was succeeded by the contingency school, which is founded on some of its principles.

The contingency school focused on applying management practice according to individual situational factors, including external environment, rather than one particular way of managing. It has been applied primarily to areas such as job design, motivation and optimizing organisational structure.

Learning Bite:
To what extent are you aware of change in management styles
over time in the organisations where you have worked? Can you
identify which schools these reflect?

From the 1970s onwards, leadership has continued to evolve
and change. And so leadership theories have continued to
evolve. Some of the most influential gurus of the latter 20th
century include:

- **Kenneth Blanchard** (1939-), who developed the popular
  Situational Leadership model with Joseph Hersey and has
  written one of the bestselling books on management of all
  time – The One Minute Manager.

- **Peter Drucker** (1909-2005) developed the very popular
  theory of Management by Objectives (MBO) as a way of
  motivating and managing staff. He has also been very
  influential in the fields of management development.

- **Peter Senge** (1947-) has focused his work on
  decentralising the role of the leader in organisations to
  empower staff to achieve more.

- **John Adair** (1934-) one of the world's leading gurus on
  leadership development with the introduction of his Action
  Centred Leadership Model.

- **Tom Peters** (1942-) is acclaimed to be one of the most
  influential business thinkers and has contributed much to
  leadership through his bestselling book "In Search of
  Excellence".

- **John Kotter** (1947-) – renowned Harvard professor has
  focused on the role of leadership in achieving successful
  organisational transformation with his 8-stage change
  management model

Modern Leadership Theories

Whilst leadership theories in the early 20th century centred on the qualities of the leader, modern theories have evolved and can be categorised under eight main headings:

- **Behavioural theories** – with its roots in the behaviourism school, this leadership theory considers that great leaders develop or are made as opposed to the great leader having some innate qualities from birth. The nature vs nurture debate continues with regard to leaders with many believing that leaders are born, whilst others believe leaders are made. Behaviourists think that leaders can learn to lead.

- **Situational theories** – this theory has been popularised by Kenneth Blanchard and Joseph Hersey, whose Situational Leadership Styles Model is one of the most popular styles around. It considers that leaders weigh up situations before deciding on a course of action that is most appropriate.

- **Contingency theories** – similar to situational theories, these assume that no one style will suit all situations or all people. Variables may include the individual followers, team dynamics, the environment or the task; these are taken into account and the management style adapted accordingly.

- **Trait theories** – identify qualities and traits that have been inherited as a natural disposition for some who will develop leadership skills. It assumes certain personality traits are inherent for good leaders, but fails to explain why not everyone who possesses these traits will rise to the challenge of leadership.

- **Great Man theories** – taken from trait theories, these depict leaders as exceptional people, as heroes who have been born with leadership ability. These people are seen as being great leaders and will typically be male. This is synonymous with military leadership.

- **Participative theories** – consider that a consultative style in which the leader takes account of the views and feelings of the followers (whilst retaining overall authority) will encourage staff to feel more involved and committed to achieving the joint goals and objectives.

- **Management theories** – are based around a carrot or stick approach to management. Staff who work hard and do well will be rewarded whilst those who do not work so well are likely to be punished in some way. Also known as transactional theories, they are used in team performance and to promote productivity.

- **Relationship theories** - focus on the relationships that develop between the leader and the follower or the manager and their staff. Known as transformational theories, these are based upon leaders focusing on both team performance and achievement, as well as individuals developing their potential. They are particularly useful in implementing change.

- **Servant leadership** – identifies the leader as someone who sees their role as that of 'serving' their followers. They perceive their power as being a duty to serve their followers rather than a real desire to lead. This style is collaborative and encourages interaction, listening and team working.

- **Dispersed leadership theory** – this modern theory of leadership argues for dispersion through an organisation in so far as leaders may emerge at all levels and the role is not therefore a hierarchical one. These are leaders who are able to influence and engage others through their personal power rather than their positional authority.

Whilst this is not an exhaustive list of theories, it gives you some idea of the main different management theories. It also serves to show how the perception of leadership has changed over time veering consistently towards the more democratic, collaborative approach to gain results.

Roles and Responsibilities

So now we have some idea of leadership theories, let's examine the difference in roles.

We started with the definition of a manager as someone who is responsible for a specific set of tasks or group of people. The manager is responsible for the operational side of the business, or part of the business. This will mean ensuring everything runs smoothly on a daily basis. The role typically focuses on a day-to-day service.

We defined the role of a leader as someone who is in a superior position with the ability to influence others. Whilst a manager focuses on the operational side of a business, the leader will focus on strategic direction, vision and change, using their influence and power to implement change.

Here is perhaps the biggest difference – and the biggest challenge. Whilst leaders are focusing on where an organisation needs to be, constantly looking to the future, the managers are trying to make it happen in the present. Leaders will say "this is where we are going" and managers will ask "how are we going to get there?".

John Kotter probably put this into words best with his quote "Management involves coping with complexity. Leadership involves coping with change"[v].

So let's look at the different responsibilities of both the manager and the leader to understand the difference in the roles:

Role of the Manager	Role of the Leader
Organising people, workload and resources	Defining direction
Planning and budgeting	Aligning people
Communicating and informing	Motivating and inspiring
Solving problems	Sharing a vision
Resolving conflicts	Establishing support
Managing people	Creating forward momentum
Managing a service, project or task	Empowering and enabling

Role of the Manager

So the role of the manager is operational and involved. Let's look in more detail at what each of these areas involve:

- **Organising people and workload** - this includes ensuring staff cover, assigning shifts and working patterns, and maintaining holiday, sickness and absence records. This requires an understanding of the staff in terms of capability, experience, knowledge, skill and attitude. It also requires knowledge of the workload and the tasks involved for all staff for whom the manager is responsible.

- **Organising resources** – this means allocating resources so that staff can do their job. Although this will depend on staff roles, it is likely to include their working space, storage, access to computers, printers and other equipment, stationery, specialist requirements (for example, safety equipment). The manager needs to ensure that the resources are available and sufficient.

- **Planning and budgeting** – this involves planning what is required to meet the demands of the service or project, forecasting output based on available resource and planning achievement of targets, objectives and aims. Some managers may be budget holders – this may mean managing all or part of a budget, acting as signatory, controlling the finances and understanding the financial aspects of the department.

- **Communicating and informing** – this means briefing and communicating as appropriate to staff, colleagues and customers. Providing information for staff at the right level to allow them to be able to fulfil their roles is a vital part of management. Briefing staff about aims, objectives, policies, procedures, working practices and changes is also essential in building staff capabilities and developing trust in a team.

- **Solving problems** – these will range from small-scale problems on a day-to-day basis to larger scale problems associated with implementing change, service improvement and restructure. A solid understanding of the problem solving process and a direct approach is required.

- **Resolving conflict** – this will typically be associated with conflict in teams arising out of personality differences, attitudes and team dynamics which the manager needs to resolve quickly and effectively to prevent longer-term problems in team working. However, managers will also encounter conflicts between the demands placed on them through targets and the resources / time available to meet them.

- **Managing people** – this is the largest and most difficult area for all managers. It begins with job design and goes through a continuous cycle of recruitment, induction, performance management, development and discipline. However, it also involves building the team, understanding individuals, influencing others, and motivating and inspiring people. This is a brief description of managing people – there is a whole chapter devoted to it later..

- **Managing a service, project or task** – task management is very different to people management requiring a different approach and different set of skills. Project management is about ensuring the objectives of the project (task or service) are met in the most efficient and effective way.

We will look at some of these areas in a lot more detail in following chapters, but this gives you a flavour of the role of the manager.

Learning Bite:
Which of the areas are most relevant to YOU in your role? How effective are you in these areas? Do you have preferences for some responsibilities over others? If so, which are they?

Role of the Leader

Whilst the manager is focusing on the present, the leader is constantly looking to the future. Never content with standing still, an effective leader will constantly be seeking ways to challenge the status quo and do more. This may be in terms of growing a business, outdoing the competition, diversifying into other areas or transforming the business. So the role involves:

- **Defining direction** – leaders are visionary and strategic. They are not interested in where they are, they are constantly looking at where they need to be. It is not sufficient to have a vision; a leader needs to have a strong sense of realism to be able to define the direction and the goal.

- **Aligning people** – no leader is a leader without followers. Influencing people to understand the direction and want to follow is a mark of a true leader. The US President, Harry Truman, said that "a great leader is a man who has the ability to get other people to do what they don't want to do and like it", which illustrates the power of leadership in influencing others.

- **Motivating and Inspiring** – through action and words, a leader will motivate and inspire people to want to achieve a vision or a goal. Another US President, John Quincy Adams put this simply, "If your actions inspire others to dream more, learn more, do more and become more, you are a leader".

- **Sharing a vision** – it is not enough to have a vision and a strategy, a leader needs to be able to share this through excellent communication skills. He will communicate with passion to inspire and motivate others to want to achieve the objectives and to turn the vision into reality.

- **Establishing support** – through communication, through listening to people and through understanding, a leader will establish support for the vision. This support is essential as leaders do not usually possess the skills and knowledge to achieve the vision alone. This is where the manager and the people are needed. Support can only be established through effective communication, through trust and mutual respect.

- **Creating forward momentum** – we have established that leadership is about change and to implement change effectively, a leader needs to create forward momentum and maintain that momentum through times of difficulty and stagnation.

- **Empowering and enabling** – one way leaders achieve their vision and attain their goals is through people. Empowering people to act and to take control to enable them to generate short term wins will help them to see the benefit of change. They will feel more involved, more motivated and part of the success.

Learning Bite:
Consider the role of the leader above and identify areas where you believe you fulfil these responsibilities either in your current role or previous roles.

Qualities

A lot of research has been done into the qualities of leadership. There are on-going debates on whether leaders are born or made and leadership qualities and characteristics form part of this discussion. However, little research has been done into the qualities of managers. Let's now take a look at the qualities of both:

Qualities of the Manager	Qualities of the Leader
Self-motivated	Self-motivated
Well-organised	Passionate
Reliable and dependable	Inspirational
Ability to resolve conflict and problems	Visionary
A team player	Decisive
Good communicator	Excellent communicator
Flexible and adaptable	Comfortable with change and ambiguity
Interested in people	Able to challenge the status quo
Able to manage change	Strategic thinkers

So we can see that some of the qualities are shared, However, where the manager is focused on people, the leader is focused on success and change.

Does this mean that a good manager cannot be a good leader? Definitely not! The ability to lead comes not from a skill-set but from a passion for success, a vision and a strategy to achieve that vision. All managers and leaders should be role models leading the way through example.

What additional qualities would you include for managers and leaders? Which are the most important for each, in your view?

The debate whether leaders are 'born' or 'made' continues, as it has for over 50 years. Some believe that leadership ability is innate and leaders will have something in their personality from birth that inspires them to succeed. Others believe that it is experience and how individuals develop through life that is credited with their success..

Looking at children in the playground, leaders emerge and other children follow. These children have been given no leadership training and yet are seen by their peers as 'leaders' – so how can we explain this? Studies of identical twins[vi] show that one third are 'born' leaders (due to genetics) and two thirds are 'made'. This would credit the theory that leaders can be made given the opportunity, the experience and the desire. However, of the third born, there is no indication of how many aspire or desire a leadership role. For many the desire will remain dormant and the leader within will not emerge.

What is your view of the 'nature vs nurture' debate on leadership? Can you offer examples to substantiate this view?

So now we have taken a look at management theories and the roles of the manager and the leader, let's take a look at management styles.

Management Styles

Management styles dictate the way that an individual will manage both staff and tasks. However, a manager's style is complex and composed of many different elements. Although personality type plays a part in the management style, this only accounts for 30% of it (Tett et al, 1991).

A large part of a manager's behaviour within the role is discretionary and effective performance is shaped by factors other than personality, for example their perception of their role, the power within that role and strategies that they develop to 'manage' their position.

These strategies are driven by underlying needs which in turn are influenced by different motivational factors, for example power, achievement and affiliation. The desire to meet internal motivational needs will drive the individual's preference for types of role and ways to adapt to the role and working environment.

Other influences extrinsic to the manager will also have an impact on the management style. These include:

- **Organisation and the culture** – each organisation has a different 'culture', much of which is intangible. This will include the organisational goals, mission statement, values and beliefs, the positional power and level of responsibility granted to its managers, the expectations placed on staff and the support structure.

- **Individual experience** – types of management, work and life experience will influence an individual's management style. It takes into account the knowledge, skills and competency within the role. Confidence and attitude will also play a part.

- **Situation** – different teams require different types of leadership style. Different people within a team will also require varying degrees of management at different times. Each situation will require a different type of management.

Figure 1 shows the different factors influencing your management style:

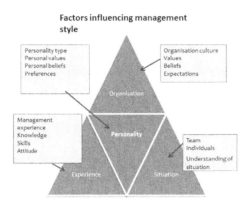

Factors influencing management style

By management style, we mean the way a manager will manage people and situations. It is their own unique approach composed of a number of different skills, experience and knowledge.

The management style tends to be based around one of five main types:

- **Autocratic** – a directive style in which the manager takes control, provides direction, gives commands and assumes responsibility. This is a traditional style successful at the turn of the 20th century and not as popular now. It is a style which presumes employees have low will and need direction without the opportunity for employees to give their views and opinions.

- **Democratic** – the antithesis to autocratic management, this offers the opportunity of full consultation with employees, valuing their opinions and basing decisions on staff input as much as the manager's own view. This is popular today in many organisations (although less so in the public sector).

- **Laissez-faire** – from the French term, this literally means 'let them get on with it'. This is a very democratic style of management, usually referred to as a delegating or joining style, in which the manager will work alongside staff and all decisions are taken together with the manager having no more or less authority than their staff.

- **Bureaucratic** – based around the need for transparency and adherence to policies, practice, processes and standards, this is typically found in public sector organisations which have a role culture. It is not a popular style; however, it is essential where there is high accountability and the consequences of malpractice may be severe.

- **Paternalistic** – a misnamed style as it implies a nurturing and altruistic style to management. However, this style does fall between autocratic and democratic, recognising the need for employee involvement with the manager retaining authority and decision-making powers. It offers a paternalistic approach through the inclusion of staff views in final decisions.

Learning Bite:
Can you identify organisations in which each style is a more typical part of the culture?

Based on these different management styles and different theories, a plethora of models has developed looking at the different ways we manage..

The most popular management style models are probably:

- Situational Leadership from Blanchard and Hersey

- Leadership Continuum developed by Robert Tannabaum and Warren Schmidt (1953, 1973)

- Action Centred leadership (also known as Functional Leadership) from John Adair

- Management by Walking Around (MBWA) popularised by Edward Deming

- Theory X and Theory Y developed by Douglas McGregor

Situational Leadership

Situational leadership was developed by Ken Blanchard and Peter Hersey during the 1970s. They believed that there was no particular 'best' style of leadership and that the most effective leaders adapted their style according to the task and the maturity of the people they manage. They identified four leadership styles which may be applied in different situations. They then considered the different levels of maturity of the team to further identify the appropriate style.[vii].

They categorised leadership style based on the task behaviour and the relationship behaviour and classified these as four behaviours, S1 through to S4, stressing that no one style is better than another. The four styles are:

- **S1 – Directive** – this top-down management style has mainly one-way communication. Staff roles are defined for them in terms of job description, objectives, tasks and responsibilities. It is the manager/leader who decides how things are going to be done, by whom, when and where. Staff have very little input. This may be seen as a dictatorial style of management where the leader assumes all of the responsibility for the task and the team

- **S2 – Coaching** – this is still a directive style of leadership; however, there is much more support for the team and individuals. Teams are encouraged to put forward their views, although the leader will still make the final decisions. There is more two-way communication and the team is influenced by a 'selling' approach as the leader explains decisions.

- **S3 – Supporting** – this is low-directive although very supportive. The team will have more influence and power and the leader will provide support at both an emotional and work level. The decision-making is shared although the leader still retains overall authority. The team will feel more empowered and more involved. They are inclined to organise themselves in terms of roles, responsibilities and duties which is then agreed by the manager.

S4 – Delegating – this style is very democratic and the leader delegates responsibility to the team. The team support each other and the structure of the team comes from the people themselves. Roles and responsibilities are set by the staff and not defined by the manager. The manager takes a back seat and the leadership of the team is bottom-up. This style works well with mature, experienced staff who work autonomously in their role - the leader's role is more of a monitoring role.

Figure 2 shows the different styles of situational leadership:

Learning Bite:
Can you identify different situations when each style may be preferred?

The maturity and ability of staff play an important part in identifying the most appropriate and effective style of leadership. Blanchard and Hersey identified four categories of staff based on their level of maturity:

- **M1** – these are staff who have a low level of ability in the specific task and are not particularly well motivated

- **M2** – applies to staff who may not have the ability but are usually motivated, willing to work hard and to learn

- **M3** – refers to people who have the ability to do the task but may lack the motivation or confidence to be effective. They therefore require a higher level of emotional support

- **M4** – refers to staff who are very capable, who need little direction and are highly motivated. They are confident and need little (if any) leadership intervention

Use of the appropriate style is very important, taking account of the situation and the staff themselves. Using the wrong style will be ineffective and lead to problems in demotivation, poor productivity and poor relationships.

Hersey believed that a leader's high expectation of a team will usually result in high performance, whilst a leader's low expectations of a team will typically result in lower performance and productivity. [viii]

Blanchard further defined the levels of maturity as levels of dependency: [ix]

- **D1** – low skill and low will

- **D2** – low skill and high will

- **D3** – high skill and low will

- **D4** – high skill and high will

Whilst situational leadership is one of the most reliable ways of assessing and matching leadership style to the task and the staff, there remains one problem. Not every leader finds it easy to adopt different styles and most will admit to a preference for a particular style of leadership. Those who have a natural preference for a 'directive' style of management will find it hard to adopt a 'delegating' style for fear of losing control of a situation. The same applies to those who prefer to take a more laissez-faire approach to management and will therefore find it more challenging to adopt a 'directive' style.

Self-awareness helps to establish your preferred style of management, consider when this is most effective and identify ways to develop the other styles for a more balanced approach to leadership overall.

Leadership Style Questionnaire

This questionnaire will provide you with an insight into your leadership style. Although your style will vary according to different factors, this will give you an idea of your preferred style. For each of the statements, please rate your normal reaction:

1 – never   2 – rarely   3 – frequently   4 – very often
    5 – almost always

	Statement	Your score				
1.	I do not believe in involving my staff in decision making	1	2	3	4	5
2.	Staff play a major part in all team decisions	1	2	3	4	5
3.	Although I make the final decision, I invite opinions from some staff	1	2	3	4	5
4.	All decisions must have the approval of each team member	1	2	3	4	5
5.	It is important to share the vision and objectives with staff	1	2	3	4	5
6.	I tell my staff what to do and I do not expect to be questioned	1	2	3	4	5
7.	Staff should plan their own work to achieve objectives	1	2	3	4	5
8.	I ask for staff views and ideas in most aspects of work	1	2	3	4	5
9.	I always explain to staff why we need to do things a certain way	1	2	3	4	5
10.	New staff must check with me before making decisions	1	2	3	4	5

11.	I discuss all changes with staff before initiating action	1	2	3	4	5
12.	All changes are discussed and agreed as a team	1	2	3	4	5
13.	My team create their own objectives and goals	1	2	3	4	5
14.	I encourage and support my staff's achievements	1	2	3	4	5
15.	The power of my management position is important to me	1	2	3	4	5
16.	I work with my staff to resolve any differences or problems	1	2	3	4	5
17.	The power of my position is necessary in helping staff to develop	1	2	3	4	5
18.	My team members establish their own standards	1	2	3	4	5
19.	I believe my staff should take responsibility for their own work	1	2	3	4	5
20	Staff need direction and discipline to achieve objectives	1	2	3	4	5
21.	All staff must understand policies and procedures	1	2	3	4	5
22.	Regular meetings are important in understanding staff needs	1	2	3	4	5
23.	I like all staff to take a turn in chairing team meetings	1	2	3	4	5
24.	Meetings are important for open discussion	1	2	3	4	5
25.	Staff need guidance to develop their full	1	2	3	4	5

	potential					
26.	I prefer staff to report back to me after completing each piece of work	1	2	3	4	5
27.	I like my staff to use their initiative in problem solving	1	2	3	4	5
28.	It is up to each individual to ensure they complete their work goals	1	2	3	4	5
29.	All my staff have clear objectives for each aspect of their role	1	2	3	4	5
30.	It is up to each individual to determine what has to be done	1	2	3	4	5
31.	I give my staff as much time and support as possible to achieve goals	1	2	3	4	5
32.	I believe staff have the ability to develop given appropriate guidance	1	2	3	4	5

Now mark your scores against the relevant statement numbers in the grid below and add your totals for each column:

1	3	2	4
6	5	8	7
10	9	11	12
15	14	16	13
20	17	19	18
21	22	23	24
26	25	27	28
29	32	31	30
Total **Directive**	*Total* **Coaching**	*Total* **Supporting**	*Total* **Delegating**

Leadership Continuum

Tannabaum and Schmidt developed the leadership continuum which looked at leadership style along a continuum with autocratic / directive at one end and democratic / laissez-faire at the other end[x]. The emphasis on their leadership model was the use of manager's authority gradually devolving to the staff over time as the team developed maturity, competency and capability. Although the natural trend is for less management intervention and more subordinate freedom over time, the manager would re-establish control if situation or necessity required.

Figure 3 below shows the different levels of authority and impact on staff

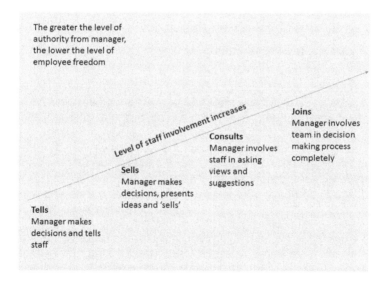

The relationship between this leadership continuum and situational leadership is evident in the movement from autocratic to democratic leadership.

Action Centred Leadership

John Adair set down his ideas on "**action-centred leadership**" or **"functional leadership"**. He developed his leadership model whilst lecturing at Sandhurst Royal Military Academy.[xi]

This approach focuses attention on the functions of leadership and believes that leadership skills can be learnt. Adair believes that leadership is more a question of appropriate behaviour than of personality and stated that the effectiveness of the leader is dependent upon meeting three areas of need within the work:

- **Task functions (needs)** – define and achieve the common task

- **Team functions (needs)** – build and maintain the team

- **Individual functions (needs)** – satisfy and develop the individuals within the team

Adair believes that there needs to be a balance between the three different needs. Too much attention on the task will lead to demoralised staff, in turn leading to lower productivity and efficiency. Too much attention on the team may mean that the needs of the task are not fulfilled and that members of the team may feel their individuality is threatened. Too much attention on individual members will provoke competition and ill-feeling within the team.

As a manager the task involves identifying the objective, defining the direction and activity required before allocating resources (people, financial, systems, tools) and developing a plan and strategy. This will also require setting the quality standards, timeframe and schedule. For the task to be completed satisfactorily the manager will need to monitor and review progress, adjusting the plan as necessary.

The manager's responsibilities for the team include developing the team in terms of establishing roles, ground rules, objectives, performance standards, team culture and synergy. This will involve resolving conflicts, maintaining discipline, providing feedback, appraising the team performance and developing the team in terms of skills, morale and cooperation.

For each individual, the manager needs to understand their unique contribution in terms of skill, attitude, knowledge, experience, potential and role within the team. The manager will be responsible for providing guidance, advice, support, recognition and feedback on an individual basis through formal and informal appraisal and assessment, as well as considering the individual development needs.

Figure 4 below shows John Adair's Action Centred leadership model

Action Centred / Functional Leadership

Three circles model TM John Adair

Management by Walking Around (MBWA)

This style of management is based around the idea that managers should reserve time to walk around the different areas in the workplace to be seen as available. It encourages open discussion with staff, offers networking opportunity and makes for a more informal culture. Initially some staff were wary believing that it is a manager's way of spying and checking up on them. However, the benefits of having managers easily accessible, available for listening and providing advice on-the-spot outweigh employee cynicism.

The benefits for managers of being able to transmit organisational values to staff on the ground floor in an informal way is of great value to all staff, particularly in times of stress when it is felt that the problems are shared and understood. It was popularised by Edward Deming who believed that:

> "If you wait for people to come to you, you'll only get small problems. You must go and find them. The big problems are where people don't realise they have one in the first place."

In the late 1980s and early 1990s this open style of management was successfully employed by Bill Hewlett and Dave Packard in the growth period of Hewlett-Packard and was widely copied by other organisations.

Theory X and Theory Y

In his book 'The Human Side of Enterprise'[xii] Douglas McGregor developed the Theory X and Theory Y of management which has also been used extensively in motivation. These are two different styles and are not opposing ends of continua.

The Theory X manager believes that workers are naturally lazy and will avoid work if it is possible. Their motivation is money rather than the work itself and therefore these people need to be closely supervised and their work monitored. This results in a narrow span of control for managers and a hierarchical structure.

The Theory X manager believes it is their role to structure, organise, control and direct staff, managing under close observation and use of systems. The working culture will be repressive and controlling with limited opportunity for creativity and energy to flourish. This type of manager will frequently look to attribute blame to staff where there are failures or problems.

The Theory Y manager has the opposite view believing that workers are naturally self-motivated, ambitious and self-disciplined. Where the right working conditions with appropriate resources are available, people will work well and productively with little management intervention as their motivation comes from their job satisfaction. This style generates an empowering culture in which staff develop and service improvements result. The Theory Y manager will create and develop a trusting culture with open communication resulting in increased motivation and productivity.

Whilst the Theory X manager has been linked to an authoritarian and directive style of management, the Theory Y is likened to the participative and collaborative style. The Theory Y style of management is more popular in most industries today as the value of human relations is better understood and valued. Most managers, however, will see the value of both styles and are unlikely to be completely one or the other. As individuals we will have a preference for being managed by a Theory X or Theory Y type manager and problems will frequently result where the opposing behaviours are stronger.

This provides you with an overview of the most popular management styles. There are many different models to choose from and apply to different working environments.

The Management Wheel

We have looked at the roles of the leader and manager and we have identified different styles applicable in different ways. However, the styles we have looked at focus on the outward side of leadership – the public face of the manager. They do not take account of the internal aspect of management – the private face of the manager. Yet a manager needs to be able to manage themself before having the ability to be a truly effective manager or leader.

The management wheel has been developed to identify the three key areas of management:

- Personal management

- People management

- Task management

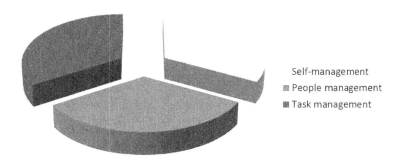

Self-management

People management

Task management

Every person is an individual with their own personality which will affect their behaviour and ability as a leader. Some managers will be more organised than others and this section (self-management) of the wheel will be larger. For other managers, task management will be their preferred option as they may be driven by targets, goals and deadlines. The key is to understand your own preferences, to increase your self-awareness, build on your strengths and develop weaker areas to become a more rounded, well-balanced leader.

Within each area are a number of spokes identifying key skills, knowledge and competencies.

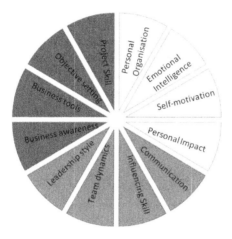

No one area is more important than another, although the role and responsibilities of the post may dictate greater need for skills in one area or another, for example project management.

Research carried out in January 2012[xiii] showed that 56% of respondents showed greater skill in people management, whilst 33% believed that personal management was their stronger area. Just 11% found task management as their higher skill area.

Personal Management

What do we mean by 'personal management'? This takes account of the personal aspects, how we manage ourselves, our time, our workload. It covers the following areas:

- **Self-motivation** - how well we are motivated (and self-disciplined) in our approach to our work. This covers setting objectives for ourselves and reviewing our progress.

- **Self-awareness** – this is about knowing ourselves, understanding our personal drivers, values, morals and beliefs. It is about understanding areas where we shine and other areas where we need to develop ourselves or our strategies. It is about identifying our sense of self and continually developing. This is probably the most important area and the one least understood.

- **Personal impact** – understanding how you come across to others, how others perceive you and how you can manage this perception.

- **Self-motivation** – understanding what drives you as a person. Identifying what is important to you, how you are motivated and how you can use this in different situations.

- **Emotional management** – understanding how we will react in different situations and learning how to manage our emotions to protect ourselves and to maximise opportunities.

- **Stress management** – recognising and understanding our stress triggers, finding ways to balance the different pressures to optimise performance.

- **Personal organisation** - how well we manage our time, the strategies we adopt for prioritising and getting the work done. It identifies our attitude towards timeliness and consideration for others' time. It also considers how we use our resources, our organisation and tidiness, and how effective we are at avoiding procrastination and achieving results.

Self-awareness is the key to a better understanding of self. We may uncover things we may not like about ourselves and this will help us to further understand the impact we have on others and how we can manage that.

We will look at the different topics of personal management later in this book and identify tools and strategies for you to develop yourself.

People Management

Most people will have a preference for either task or people, although this does not mean you cannot learn the skills for both. People management is one of the most enjoyable and challenging aspects of management. It covers a multitude of topics, particularly:

- **Team dynamics** – understanding the group dynamics and building the team in terms of roles, responsibilities, performance, skills, experience and synergy.

- **Developing individuals** – through regular feedback, appraisal, objective setting, personal development planning and coaching. This will also include providing support, advice and guidance through change and difficult situations.

- **Conflict management** – managing conflict intra-team and with other staff in an organisation, using conflict as a learning opportunity.

- **Motivating staff** - inspiring them to achieve objectives and improve productivity.

- **Influencing people** – developing strategies to influence, persuade and negotiate with people.

- **Encouraging creativity** and innovation amongst staff through involvement in problem solving and decision making.

- **Establishing a culture of trust** and confidence in which staff feel valued, involved and empowered.

- **Communicating** – providing information to the team, colleagues and customers as required in the appropriate format and at the relevant time.

- **Managing change** – understanding the impact of change on people and managing change accordingly.

We will look at each of these areas in more detail later in the book.

Task Management

Task management is a part of every manager's role as the manager is achieving the task or providing a service through the staff. Whilst it is difficult to distinguish responsibilities between task and people, the following activities are more task-oriented:

- **Business Awareness** – understanding the business and organisation you are working in, having a good understanding of the vision, objectives and mission for the company and able to identify ways to develop and improve the business.

- **Problem solving** – using different techniques and tools to understand and solve problems.

- **Change management** – developing an understanding of the tools involved in planning and managing change in an organisation.

- **Business tools** – developing an awareness of the different business tools to help in the role.

Before you complete the questionnaire, consider where your
strengths lie in terms of the management wheel. Where are you
likely to be strongest? Which is your weaker area? How does
this impact on your current role?

Now turn the page to assess your competence in each of the
three areas.

Management Wheel Questionnaire

Each of the following statements represents aspects of management behaviour.
For each identify the extent to which it applies to you.

5 – Strongly agree; 4 – Agree; 3 – Partly agree; 2 –Disagree; 1 – Strongly disagree;

1   All staff should have regular appraisals

2   Analysing problems is one of my strengths

3   Change and service improvement are essential to stay ahead of the competition

4   Creativity is important and I encourage my staff and colleagues to be innovative

5   Effective team working is critical in providing a good service

6   Everyone should be given the opportunity to develop their full potential

7   I am motivated by challenging tasks and stretching objectives

8   I am naturally self-motivated

9   I believe my staff and working colleagues are able to trust and confide in me

10   I encourage my staff to participate in decision making

11   I enjoy concentrating on the details of a complex task

12   I enjoy finding out about new working practices and considering how to implement them

13   I expect all my staff to follow procedures and protocols

closely

14	I expect my staff to be professional in the workplace and leave personal problems at home
15	I find it easy to influence people around to my way of thinking
16	I have a good understanding of professional boundaries and respect these in the workplace
17	I have my own personal development plan
18	I respect other people who have different values to mine
19	I set myself achievable targets regularly
20	I trust my staff to make the right decisions
21	I try to implement other people's ideas where possible
22	I try to resolve conflict with others and especially in teams
23	I understand my stress triggers and have coping strategies
24	I understand the impact I have on other people and I try to manage this appropriately
25	I use lists and other tools to make sure I stay in control of my workload
26	I am rarely late for meetings and appointments
27	It is important to monitor other people's objectives
28	Maintaining a motivated team is very important to me
29	Managing by objectives is the best way to motivate staff productivity
30	My own professionalism is very important
31	My values and morals are very important to me
32	My working environment is tidy and well organised
33	Project plans and Gantt charts are essential in

managing a service or project

34   Quality is important in all aspects of work

35   The customer is the most important person in any
organisation

36   The task is the most important part of the role and must
always take priority

Now mark the questionnaire to find out your scores.

Circle the statement numbers for 8, 9, 16, 17, 19, 24, 25, 26, 30,
31 and 32

Tick the statement numbers for 1, 4, 5, 6, 10, 14, 15, 18, 20, 21,
22 and 28

Add the scores for the circled statements – this is your self-
management score

Add the scores for the ticked statements – this is your people
management score

Add the scores for all remaining statements – this is your task
management score

        Self-Management

        People Management

        Task Management

Learning Bite:
Now look back at the previous learning point. Is your wheel as
you would have predicted? How may this impact on you in your
role? Can you identify areas for development?

Personal Management

We are now going to look at the main topics of personal management and consider strategies and ways to help you to develop further in this area.

Self-Awareness

Personal management begins with understanding ourselves, identifying what drives us, what inspires us and what motivates us. You can begin by considering what is important to you:

- **Values** – these are what we hold close to us. They are the moral code we live by and may have been influenced by our upbringing, our childhood, influential people in our lives (parents, siblings, mentors, teachers), our culture and our experience. We each have ideas of what is right and what is wrong – it is our internal law by which we work and live.

- **Beliefs** – what we believe to be true. Our beliefs influence the way we act, the way we think, the way we interpret events and the way we perceive others. Different types of beliefs include:

    o **Positive beliefs** – which will carry a positive connotation that we believe we have the power and can do something

    o **Limiting beliefs** – which will limit the extent we are likely to achieve and have an impact on our self-confidence and esteem

    o **Negative beliefs** – our lack of belief in ourselves and our ability to carry out certain tasks or to achieve certain goals

- **Memories** – some memories will be very vivid, either negative or positive, and may have an influence on the way we behave now because of the impact of the past.

These values, beliefs and memories will influence the way you live and work – they define who you are, they build your identity and help you to develop relationships with others. We are naturally drawn to others who share our beliefs and values, for example, political or religious groups. We are comfortable around them as we have a shared rapport.

Learning Bite: *Consider how well you understand yourself. Make a note of your values and beliefs. How do these influence you in your work?*

One tool that can help us to find out more about ourselves is the Johari Window, developed by Joseph Ingham and Harry Luft in the 1950s[xiv]. It identifies four quadrants which consider the four aspects of personality. Charles Handy[xv] considers this as the Johari house with four rooms, each with its own characteristics as shown in figure 7 below:

Public Arena – known to self and others	Private Self – known only to self
Blind Spot – known to others and unknown to self	Hidden – unknown to others and self

The private self is the you that you know and choose not to show to others. It may include your secret hopes, thoughts, dreams and plans. This is your inner voice.

The public arena is the area that you and others see. It is the face you put on for the rest of the world and part of this may be influenced by how you want others to perceive you as a person.

The blind spot is the part of you that others see but of which you are blissfully unaware. Whilst these may be negative traits that we choose not to see, they may also be positive qualities of which we are not aware.

The hidden area is the unknown – this is the part of you that neither you nor others have considered or explored. It may include hidden qualities, skills or traits which have yet to come to the fore through opportunity and experience.

The windows may not all be the same size – this will vary according to the individual as some people are much more private and introvert, whilst others are more public and extrovert.

As a tool, it will help you to assess your own qualities. As a manager it helps you to promote self-awareness in your staff, to give individuals feedback to better understand their blind spots and to promote opportunities for them to explore the hidden facets of their personalities..

Self-awareness is created through a variety of different ways including questionnaires, reflection, feedback and continued development.

Questionnaires - assess you in different ways. There are many of these including personality tests, management style questionnaires (you have already completed a couple of these in this book), psychometric questionnaires and team-role preference questionnaires. Some are better than others. All will help you to build up a picture of yourself and increase your self-awareness

Reflection - in many professions (nursing and teaching for example), reflection is a key component of the learning. It is extensively found in practice-based professional settings and is used to learn from experience. Reflective practice is the term used to encourage experiential learning and practice adaptation and modification in different contexts. Reflection can help you to develop professionally and personally. One of the best ways of reflecting is to keep a reflective journal or diary in which you note experiences and events from which you can learn. Although this may seem tedious initially, it soon becomes easier as you begin to appreciate the value.

There are a variety of different models for reflection. Gibb's model of reflection (1988)[xvi] is one of the most effective as it has six distinct stages for individuals to work through as shown in Figure 8 below:

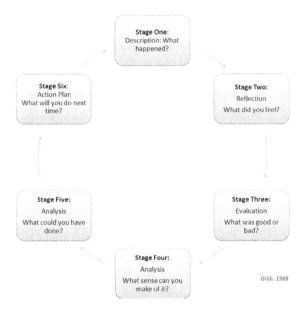

Gibb, 1988

Feedback – feedback from others allows us to find out things we may not have been aware of, or may have been aware of and needed reinforcement. When properly done, feedback can be a powerful way of developing professionally and personally although a certain level of trust between the giver and recipient is needed for the feedback to be credible. Receiving feedback is only one part of the process; the recipient needs to take the feedback on board – this may not always be easy as we frequently see it as a personal criticism. Maintaining an open mind, remembering that feedback is intended to help us develop, will help. The learning comes from the exploration of alternatives and the willingness to change.

Development – whatever your role you need to continue to develop, to explore new techniques and strategies for doing things differently. As a manager, you are responsible for advising on development for your staff. You are also responsible for ensuring you have a personal development plan. This may be focused on developing new knowledge and skills, or on maintaining current and up-to-date awareness. The most self-aware managers are those with a personal development plan who are constantly developing in different areas.

Learning Bite:
Do you have a personal development plan for yourself? If not, consider two areas you need to develop over the next three months and identify actions to take.

Personal Impact

"It takes 30 seconds to make an impact" (Albert Mehrabian[xvii]). Your impact and presence control others' perceptions of you as an individual, your knowledge, your skills and your qualities. You therefore need to make the right impression as you never get a second chance to make a first impression. People judge you by what you look like, how you dress, your body language and how you behave – this is frequently a sub-conscious judgement. This is based on what they see, what you do and how you do it, although what people see accounts for 60% and what you actually do only accounts for 10%.

Now you have a better understanding of self-awareness and how it is important, you can build on that self-knowledge. Personal impact is about:

- Body language – non-verbal communication

- Your personal brand (packaged to reflect your identity)

- Adaptation to your environment, different situations and people

Start by thinking about the external you. Consider the following questions to assess the impact you have on others:

- Do you make eye contact with other people? Does this depend on situation / the other person?

- Do you greet people with a smile?

- Are you naturally a happy, energetic person? Or a quiet, reflective person? Or do you have a 'can't be bothered' attitude about you? Do you come across as aggressive or intimidating to others?

- Do you reach out to shake hands with people when you meet them?

- Do you consider how you come across to others in different situations?

- Do you give much attention to your attire? Do you dress differently according to occasion and situation?

- Do you consider how other people are dressed?

- Do you sometimes feel uncomfortable around people and not sure about your body language?

- Do you like to start the conversation or do you prefer someone else to begin talking?

- Do you listen attentively and ask questions of others?

- Are you generally easy-going and find people get on well with you?

- Do you generally find it difficult to go up to people you don't know?

Let's examine what influences others' perception of you:

Energy and enthusiasm

Your sense of energy and enthusiasm comes across through
your body language and your approach to people. People
naturally gravitate towards happier, enthusiastic people who
exude energy. This does not mean that quiet, reflective people
will put others off. It may just take longer to fully engage with
them and build the rapport.

Posture

If your posture is upright and confident, you will come across as
confident and people will engage with you and trust you. People
who slouch create a 'don't care' impression which discourages
others. The correct posture will also help you feel more
confident.

Consider the way you shake hands – a firm handshake inspires
confidence, a bone-cruncher implies aggressiveness and a wet
fish gives the impression of not caring.

Part of our posture and our influence over others comes from
how we occupy the space around us. We all have our own
personal comfort zones and we feel threatened by anyone who
invades our personal space[xviii]. We begin to feel nervous,
slightly intimidated and we are not communicating at our best.
Some people will be aware of this and deliberately use it to their
advantage. Others are 'kinaesthetic' and feel more comfortable
standing close to you. If you are feeling uncomfortable, simply
step away a little. Our comfort zones can be split into three
zones:

- *Intimate zone* – surrounds us for between 15-45cm; only lovers, parents, children and very close friends are permitted within this zone

- *Personal zone* – up to 1m; comfortable with friends, associates and colleagues. Sometimes called the 'party' zone as socialising is frequently in this zone because of space limitations

- *Social zone* – extends beyond 1m and includes people we don't know well, we don't like or don't feel comfortable with

We like to own the territory around us and we don't like it invaded. People who stand close to us (in our intimate zone) are indirectly threatening to us; they make us feel uncomfortable. Zones vary according to country and culture. This territorial ownership is not limited to our person. We extend it to our possessions and family. We feel resentful if we return to find someone sitting in our chair at our desk as we see this as an invasion of our personal space. We don't like it when someone else uses our mug in the communal kitchen. In the same way we use furniture and other equipment to show possession and dominance in our own area. You will see people leaning against desks (or cars) to show possession and hint at their power (within their personal territory).

Learning Bite:
Think about how you use the space around you. Do you demonstrate territorial possession? How do you feel about people standing too close to you? How can you manage that?

Body Language

Body language has become increasingly popular over the last 20 years or so and is now a recognised way of communicating and impacting on others. It is all about the ability to read other people's thoughts and feelings through gestures, actions and what is left unsaid. Naturally, behaviour patterns have existed for thousands of years, but it is only the past forty years that have seen extensive research into body language. Although we have long been aware of the signals animals send to each other, as human beings we have been slow to accept the importance of body language in our daily communications with each other.

A study conducted by Albert Mehrabian [xix] in the 1960s demonstrated the value of non-verbal communication. He considered the impact of words versus vocal expression and visual impact. He concluded that

Total Liking = 7% Verbal + 38% Vocal + 55% Visual

From this study, people have concluded that around 7% of the message received comes from spoken word, 38% from verbal expression and 55% from body language. Other research found similar conclusions. These numbers emphasise the impact of body language on our communications with others and our interpersonal relationships.

We have an innate and sub-conscious ability to communicate through gestures and signals. It is also human behaviour to mirror and match each other's posture and actions if we want to gain acceptance, and conversely mis-match where we are in conflict with the other person. Although body language may differ between countries with gestures having different interpretations in different countries or cultures, much of our body language is universal, particularly in Western society. There has been much debate over whether body language is innate or learned. Certainly through studying people around us, we can develop our awareness, learn to 'read' behavioural signals and adapt our body language accordingly.

Whilst it becomes false to manipulate your body language, it can be helpful to manage it. It can provide a valuable tool in communication and it begins with understanding your own body language and the impact on others. You can then develop your awareness of others' behavioural signals to help you to 'listen' and facilitate your understanding.

Awareness of body language comes from observation and understanding the basics. Start 'people watching' to find out more about this fascinating subject and you will soon begin to understand more about the communication process.

People who are honest and open will usually have open gestures as they have nothing to hide. Open palms shows that we are prepared to be honest as we spread our hands and arms, whilst people who hide their hands are frequently trying to avoid disclosure, are concealing something or are lying. People with crossed arms or legs may be defensive and not prepared to be as honest with you, although this can sometimes be for comfort or because the person is feeling nervous or intimidated.

Hands are an excellent indicator of how a person is feeling as they are usually quite visible. We know that clenched fists express anger and the tighter they are clenched the angrier the person. People with specialist skills will frequently 'steeple' their hands in front of their faces – this indicates knowledge and understanding.   Bitten fingernails show someone is worried or nervous as does fiddling with hair or anything else that is available. Drumming fingers indicate impatience. A liar will frequently cover their mouth with their hand and will not make eye contact. Someone feeling uncomfortable may run their finger around their collar ('hot under the collar'). Those who tend to point at others are confrontational and showing a desire to control or manage the situation.

One recognised way of improving inter-personal relationships is to use mirroring and matching techniques. These can be effective when used carefully as they reflect that you are in tune with others in the group. Mirroring requires you to watch the other person's actions and body language and mirror accordingly.   Matching is less obvious and involves matching body language, for example if one person crosses their right leg over their left, you may cross your right foot over your left. This is less intrusive and has as much impact as mirroring.

In the same way that we match non-verbal behaviour, we can tune into others' talk and match their words. This means picking up on what has been said and responding with similar language and vocabulary. It shows that we are in tune with the other person and is likely to appeal at a sub-conscious level.

Self-Motivation

Self-motivation drives you to achieve. We are all motivated in different ways and you need to identify how you are motivated and what motivates you.

- **Intrinsic motivation** – internal drive that pushes you to work harder, to achieve more for your own sake and the satisfaction it brings you.

- **Extrinsic motivation** – external drive that influences our achievements. This may be carrot (reward and recognition) or stick (fear or threat). Money and promotion are two examples of extrinsic motivation. On the flip side, redundancy or bankruptcy are equally examples of extrinsic motivation.

- **Objectives** – well-thought out and planned objectives will motivate. The term 'management by objectives' (MBO) was coined by Peter Drucker[xx] as a way of motivating staff through clearly defined objectives.

Self-motivation is about having objectives to achieve, challenges to stretch you, dreams to aim for and a hunger. It is about not giving up when things are difficult and finding a way to inspire yourself. YOU are the only one that can motivate YOU. No matter how many other talents, qualities, skills and knowledge you have, without self-motivation you cannot aspire to attain more.

The following steps will help you:

- Set yourself an objective or a goal. The difference between a dream and an objective is a strategy. Define your dream as a realistic goal. Make your dream a reality by setting yourself short-term achievable objectives.

- Small steps are important. Short-term objectives are the small steps that will help you on your way. Celebrate each achievement to motivate you towards the next step.

- Be hungry – desire is not enough. You have to be really hungry to achieve it.

- Don't compare yourself to others – aim for your own objective. Other people have different goals and work towards them in different ways. Your goal is the one that is important to you. Mikhail Baryshnikov[xxi] said, "*I do not try to dance better than anyone else. I only try to dance better than myself.*"

- Keep going – even when it gets difficult – this is when you will appreciate the results most.

- Never rely on anyone else – learn to depend upon yourself for motivation. It is YOUR goal, YOUR dream, YOUR objective and YOU will enjoy the success when you achieve it.

We will look more at motivational theory in the People Management section.

Emotional Management

"For leadership positions emotional intelligence competencies account for up to 85% of what sets outstanding managers apart from the average"[xxii] (Daniel Goleman).

During the 1990s everyone began to talk about 'emotional intelligence'. Companies began to recruit for employees' interpersonal and intrapersonal skills as much as their qualifications and experience. Emotional intelligence was developed by two US psychologists, Peter Salovey and John Mayer. They identified that emotional intelligence was the possession of an emotional awareness and sensitivity about yourself and others with the aim of maximizing long-term happiness and survival. This means knowing how you and other people feel and considering what can be done about it. It is understanding what feels good, what feels bad and how to move away from bad towards good. Salovey and Mayer believed that emotional intelligence could be a learned ability to help us to manage our emotions so that they work for us and not against us.

There are various models looking at the different stages of emotional intelligence with the most well-known being that of Daniel Goleman. The models vary, but generally assume that there are four stages of emotional intelligence. These can be grouped into two areas - intrapersonal (inwardly focusing on you as an individual) and interpersonal (how we manage our relationships with others).

Figure 9 below shows the four areas of the model:

We have already explored self-awareness and the importance of understanding ourselves, how we are perceived by others, our energy levels and our inner values that guide us. This also concerns how we control our emotions. Emotional management is about understanding our emotions and feelings. This means developing an awareness of our 'hot buttons' that will trigger irrational responses and bursts of anger, emotion or stress. It is about learning to control our unproductive behaviour. To do this we need to understand the link between our interpretation of a situation or person and our response so that we can choose how to feel and how to react.

Learning Bite:
Consider your own triggers for unproductive behaviour. How can you learn to control these?

Let's look briefly at the dynamics of emotion – the ABC of our reactions:

$$A + B = C$$

A is an example of this Activating event – the trigger which will cause us to react. Now this may be a real event or an imagined event (born from insecurity or anxiety). Either way our reaction will be influenced by our beliefs.

B are the Beliefs that will influence our interpretation of an event. Beliefs come from our upbringing, the people around us and our life experiences. They will colour the way we see things and therefore affect our reaction or the consequences.

C is the Consequence or our reaction to the situation. This may be rational or it may be completely irrational. Either way it will be invoked by our beliefs and will provoke certain behaviour.

An example of this could be traffic congestion. One driver sitting in their car will be fuming at the hold-up, angry because the event is beyond their control and considering all the problems that this is going to cause them during the day. Their reaction is stressful and out of perspective. They are not helping themself – or anyone else. However, another driver sitting in the car behind in the same traffic jam may accept that the situation is beyond their control, tune in their radio and sit back to listen to the music. Therefore they are controlling their reaction to the situation and will be far calmer and relaxed once the traffic moves.

Whilst we cannot change situations, we can influence the way we react to them – we can CHOOSE how we want to behave.

The key in this model is understanding our reaction to certain situations, seeking to consider the rational responses leading to more productive behaviour rather than fearing the worst which leads to unproductive behaviour.

Emotional management is critical for every manager and leader – yet it is the area where people are likely to score lowest as it is the hardest one for us to control, particularly in situations where we feel we have no authority or control over the outcome.

Moving on to the third area of our emotional intelligence model, we need to understand our environment. At work this will include an awareness of the organisational culture, the way things are done, the people we work with and how we can empathise and develop our social awareness.

Relationship management is looking at how effective we are at building and maintaining our networks and relationships with others. How we are treated by others will depend on how we see ourselves. If we have self-confidence and high self-esteem, people will respect us more and will treat us better. Peter Honey[xxiii], a behavioural psychologist, said that "behaviour breeds behaviour" meaning that how we treat others will influence how they treat others. Take our attitude on the road as a driver. If you drive to work, you will be able to visualize the scenario: you are running late for work and as you try to pull out onto the main road, no-one will let you through. Eventually you pull into the flow of traffic – however, you are unlikely to let another driver out because nobody offered you the chance. However, taking the same scenario with someone letting you pull out into the flow of traffic straight away, you are more likely to do the same for another person. In the same way, if someone gives their seat up on the train for a less capable person, another passenger is likely to do the same. Behaviour breeds behaviour.

Emotionally intelligent managers are respected for their ability to get to know their staff, to develop trusting relationships and to coach their team effectively.

According to Goleman, emotionally intelligent people are able to interpret situations and label feelings, not people or situations, taking responsibility for these feelings and using them productively. Equally they show respect for others' feelings, rarely advise, control, criticise or blame and practise getting positive value from negative emotions. Finally, they avoid people who don't respect them, who belittle or patronise.

Learning Bite:
Consider how you assess yourself in the different areas of this emotional intelligence model. Identify ways to develop your weaker areas.

Stress Management

Stress has been defined by the Health and Safety Executive as "the adverse reaction people have to excessive pressures or other types of demand placed on them"[xxiv].

Stress is not new – psychologists have been studying different forms of stress since the 1950s. However, it has become more prevalent in recent years for two main reasons. Firstly, because stress used to be perceived as some form of mental illness which was best kept hidden as it could have a negative impact on relationships and prospects at work. Today this is not the case and people are more willing to admit to stress at work. Secondly, because the term 'stress' is much more commonly used, people are more aware of it and it has become something of a buzz word. Work related stress (WRS) in itself is not an illness. However, the psychological effects can contribute to other illnesses including back problems, heart disease and gastrointestinal illnesses.

Although typically seen as a problem, stress can be good for you. When used appropriately, stress releases creative energy enabling you to enjoy a happier and more fulfilling life. However, stress varies from one individual to another and we each have our own level of alertness at which our mind and body function best. At our peak alertness we feel energised, enthusiastic and in control, as seen in figure 10 below:

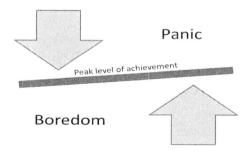

Stress is your body's physical and emotional reaction to demand
and there are several different types of stress.

Figure 11 below shows you the different types of stress:

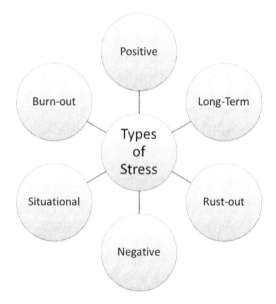

- **Positive stress** – challenges you to achieve goals and
  produce good quality work within a short timeframe. Many
  people find that positive stress is a motivator that inspires
  them to achieve deadlines and objectives.

- **Negative stress** – this is demotivating, it causes us to
  procrastinate and we become less productive and unable to
  achieve our goals or meet deadlines.

- **Short term** – usually triggered by a one-off cause (also
  known as situational stress) which will only create low
  productivity for a short period of time or in a particular

situation. This type of stress is usually only related to a particular incident and therefore dissipates quickly.

- **Long term** – usually builds up over time causing greater problems, particularly the longer it is left. If left unmanaged, long term stress becomes excessive with negative results leading to personal problems, lower productivity and ill health. It creates feelings of disempowerment and demotivation.

- **Rust-out** – this will occur where there is too little stress resulting in boredom, apathy, lethargy, low levels of energy, demotivation and lack of challenge.

- **Burn-out** – at the other extreme, this occurs when there is excessive stress resulting in the individual feeling emotionally, mentally and physically exhausted, much more likely to fall ill and be less productive at work.

So what causes stress? This will vary from person to person and also from one organisation to another. Most people will be able to identify stressful elements of their role. Sources of stress in the workplace may include:

- Being over employed – having too much to do leading to panic

- Being under employed – having too little to do, leading to lethargy

- Role confusion – lack of understanding of own role and boundaries with others

- Relationships – with staff, with peers or with higher management

- Lack of recognition – leading to feelings of inadequacy and under-valued

- Uncertainty about future – frequently due to organisational changes and the economic environment

- Lack of control – either lack of authority to carry out role effectively or lack of perceived authority

- Organisational culture – particularly where there are a lot of deadlines, key performance indicators (KPIs) or pressures

- Harassment – bullying and harassment in the workplace

Stress in personal life may be due to different factors and may include the following sources:

- Financial circumstances which may be coupled with job uncertainty

- Pace of life, particularly when trying to juggle too many commitments

- Commitments and the balance between personal life and work

- Social environment – could be due to pressures, problems or conflict between family, friends, community or the physical environment

Symptoms of stress fall into four different categories. You may experience symptoms in one or more categories:

- **Physical** – headaches, palpitations, panic attacks, twitching, allergies, frequent illness and infection, weight loss / gain and poor sleeping habits

- **Mental** – forgetfulness and absent-mindedness, inability to make decisions, frequent mistakes, poor concentration and worrying over trivial matters

- **Emotional** – irritability with others, anger and outbursts of temper or crying, loss of confidence and low self-esteem, cynicism, fear, anxiety, taking offence at minor incidents and general depression

- **Behavioural** – lack of sociability with others, sense of restlessness and inability to focus on goals, poor time management, changes in appetite and increases in smoking and alcohol-drinking, withdrawal from others, hostility towards other people and lower productivity

A survey on the quality of working life, conducted by the Chartered Institute of Personnel Development in 2006[xxv] showed alarming levels of respondents with symptoms of stress with over 55% complaining of muscle tiredness, aches, pains and constant tiredness at work. 43% admitted becoming angry with others too easily leading to workplace tensions.

Understanding our stressors and our reaction to stress is vital as a manager (and as an individual). However, we also need to consider ways that we can manage our stress so that it works for us (positive stress) rather than against us.

Quick stress reduction techniques will work for short-term, situational stress and include the following:

- Talking it through with a colleague

- A brisk walk to re-energise

- Rehydrate by drinking more water to release more energy

Longer-term stress needs longer-term techniques to manage it and will require changing habits:

- Consider your eating habits and look at adopting a healthier diet

- Incorporating more exercise into your daily routine (without excessive activity)

- Taking up yoga, pilates or meditation

- Getting more sleep

- Talking through problems and worries with another person or with the team at work

- Understanding your stressors and developing strategies to cope with them

- Redefining your work/life balance

1. **Put your problems into perspective** – few problems are truly catastrophic. Try to break big problems into small chunks which may be easier to resolve. It helps to put problems into perspective. If something is worrying you today, consider if it will still worry you tomorrow or next week, next month or next year. You will find a point when it is no longer going to worry you – so it's not worthy losing sleep over now.

2. **Change your viewpoint** – refuse to let others cause you stress. Try not to bear grudges against others and say something nice to someone else (it makes you feel better too).

3. **Find some humour** – learn to laugh more. Studies show that nursery age children laugh on average 450 times a day whilst the average adult will only laugh 15 times a day. Share a joke or find something to laugh about. Laughter is contagious and will make you and others feel better.

4. **Be nice to yourself** – learn to like yourself. Banish the inner critic and don't undermine yourself. When you make mistakes use it as a learning opportunity and look at ways to move on.

5. **Slow down** – take up a relaxing hobby, make a walk part of your daily routine, read non-work related books and use travel time to relax (and not work).

Learning Bite:
Identify your own levels of stress. Consider ways that you can bring this under control to make stress work for you.

Personal Organisation

This is possibly one of the largest areas of self-management and certainly one which creates the biggest problems for some people.

What is personal organisation?

It is the way you organise yourself, your environment, your time, your resources and your workload so that you can meet your commitments effectively. The problem with personal organisation is that everyone is different. We all have different demands on our time, both personally and professionally. We have different priorities and perceive things differently. Some people are very organised and others simply aren't. However, whilst I do not believe you can teach people time management, I do believe you can learn strategies that will help you to become better organised.

Time Management

Let's begin with time management – how we use and organise our time effectively.

What is time management?

Time management is the process for controlling your life through the way you use your time. Actively managing your time allows you to assess the values in your professional and personal life and to direct your time efforts accordingly. Effective time management enables you to balance the many pressures on your time, limit stress, be more productive at work and achieve your goals.

Time management starts with the commitment to change. Improving your time management involves better planning, learning to prioritise, delegating effectively, managing your environment, understanding yourself and identifying how you need to change your habits, routines and attitudes.

The key to successful time management is planning and then protecting the planned time. People who say that they have no time do not plan, or fail to protect planned time. If you plan what to do and when, and then stick to it, then you will have time. This involves conditioning, or re-conditioning your environment. For people who have demands placed on them by others, particularly other departments, managers or customers, time management requires diplomatically managing the expectations of others. Time management is chiefly about conditioning your environment, rather than allowing your environment to condition you. If you tolerate, and accept without question, the interruptions and demands of others then you effectively encourage these time management pressures to continue.

Stephen Covey[xxvi], author of "Seven Habits of Highly Effective People" claims the principle of good time management, which he calls the habit of personal leadership, is one of the key ingredients for successful managers.

"habit 2 - begin with the end in mind®

Covey calls this the habit of personal leadership - leading oneself towards what you consider your aims. By developing the habit of concentrating on relevant activities you will build a platform to avoid distractions and become more productive and successful.

Covey offers a lot of good advice for taking control of your time and your destiny and this begins with time management.

Eight facts about time management

1. Everyone has the same 168 hours in a week
2. Most people don't understand where their time goes
3. We usually under-estimate how long a task is going to take
4. We leave the tasks we least enjoy to the last
5. The worst time of day for staying focused is between 14.00 and 16.00
6. Research shows that you can increase personal productivity by up to 20% by improving personal time management
7. Creating goals helps us to focus on managing time

8.   People have different daily rhythms – understanding your preference helps you to plan activities accordingly[xxvii]

Over the past ten years, a number of research studies have looked at the difference that makes some of us early birds and some of us night owls. Various studies have identified that it is a genetic disposition. In 2005, the University of Surrey conducted research in this field. Around 500 people completed questionnaires about their sleep patterns which identified them either as 'larks', 'owls' or intermediate sleepers at neither extreme. They found that those who go to bed late had a 'short' version of a gene called "Period 3" while early risers had a 'long' version. The genes affect the internal body clock (circadian rhythms). Dr Simon Archer, co-author of the study said "It will be possible one day to manipulate genes to change them. But it's more likely that the findings will be used to advise people whether they are 'owls' or 'larks' and what sort of lifestyle they are suited to, such as whether they should be doing shift work for example".

By identifying our own preferred pattern, we can consider when we are going to be most effective. For example, the larks are more alert in the morning and should therefore schedule more important tasks and meetings (as far as possible) before lunch. Owls, on the other hand, are more effective later in the day and will be best using the time from mid-morning onwards for more important tasks. It therefore makes sense that we should plan the more mundane tasks for our low-energy times as these do not require high levels of energy.

Complete the questionnaire over the page to ascertain whether you are a lark, an owl or an intermediary. For each choice, circle the answer most similar to your style.

Your Personal Preference

	A	B	C
Do you need a strong coffee before you can function fully in the morning?	Usually ✓	Sometimes	Rarely
Do you fall asleep in front of the television or a book in the evening?	Rarely	Usually ✓	Sometimes
What is the worst time of day for you to stay focused?	8.00am	10.00pm ✓	6.00pm
Are you one of the first people to arrive at a party?	Never	Usually	Sometimes ✓
Do you wake in the morning keen to get on with the day ahead?	Never	Usually	Sometimes ✓
Does your alarm clock wake you in the morning?	Always ✓	Sometimes	Rarely
When do you like to get your work done?	Evening	Morning	Any time ✓
When do you like socialising with your friends best?	Evening	Weekend ✓	Don't mind
When do you prefer to eat your main meal?	After 6.00pm	Before 8.00pm ✓	Any time
If asked to attend a breakfast meeting, would your reaction be	Oh no!	Fine by me	Could we make it later? ✓
If working shifts, would you prefer	Night	Day ✓	Mixture

Mostly A – you're definitely a night owl who cannot function early in the morning and much prefers the evening. Use the time later in the day to focus on important tasks.

Mostly B – you're a lark who wakes early and wants to get on with your day. You find it difficult to focus in the evening so try to get important tasks done during the morning.

Mostly C – you're an intermediate. You don't have any real preference and can plan your day according to external requirements.

You can look at time management from a complete perspective of how you organise your life, or you can just look at your working life.

Let's focus on looking at your working life. To help you with your time management, you need to begin by identifying exactly what your role and responsibilities are. You may want to use your job description to help you with this. It is a three-stage process.

Stage One:

Start by asking yourself:

> What is the purpose of my job?
> What do I do?
> What am I hoping to achieve?

This will give you the overall purpose of your role – it should be limited to a single sentence, for example "to effectively run the print room to deliver quality output on time".

Stage Two:

Once you have identified your role, you need to look at the key responsibilities for your role. These will typically be the main areas on which you concentrate most of your time and effort towards achieving your overall purpose. You would normally have around five key areas. So ask yourself:

> What are my key responsibilities?

What are my objectives?
What deadlines do I need to meet?

Stage Three:

Lastly, you need to look at each key responsibility in turn and identify the tasks which make up each area. This will give you a role definition which clarifies your job in terms of what you are actually required to do and helps you to identify the areas where you should spend your time.

Learning Bite:
Consider your current role and define the purpose and key
responsibilities. For each of these, identify the tasks required.

Now you have your role definition and your mission, you can learn to prioritise and work towards your goals.

SMART objectives

Goals are critical to effective time management. They drive how you should be spending your time. With defined goals, you know what is most important to accomplish on a daily and weekly basis, so that you do not spend time on non-urgent tasks that do not help you achieve your top goals.

You need to review your long-term goals and priorities to be able to plan and manage your time effectively. Try looking at:

- Your organisational goals

- Your departmental goals

- Your personal goals

These goals guide your time usage in two ways:

- They allow you to identify the specific tasks that you need to pursue.

- They help you to determine which tasks you should not be pursuing.

SMART objectives help us to focus:

S	Specific
M	Measurable
A	Achievable; attainable; agreed
R	Realistic; relevant
T	Timebound

A SMART objective will encapsulate all these ingredients in one brief sentence. For example an objective may read: "To produce a monthly report by the 15th of each month on the forward load status for all staff for the next three months for the Operations Director."

Objectives should be documented in priority order and give indications of targets, goals and timeframes over an agreed period of time. Too many objectives are unrealistic and demoralising. Around ten is an acceptable amount.

Learning Bite:
Consider three SMART objectives for you to focus on over the coming week / month. Now prioritise these.

Urgency v Importance

The urgency versus importance matrix has been attributed to two very different leaders. The first was the US President Eisenhower who quoted "What is important is seldom urgent and what is urgent is seldom important" and for these reasons the following grid has frequently been called the "Eisenhower Principle" as this was how he organised his time and his duties.

Stephen Covey developed the idea further in his book "7 Habits of Highly Effective People" in 1994 and he called it "The Urgent / Important Matrix".

The concept behind the matrix is to understand which tasks are urgent, which are important and to take action accordingly. To begin, we need to differentiate between 'important' and 'urgent'.

Urgent tasks imply immediacy. There is a time limit or deadline and therefore we need to react quickly.

Important tasks are those which are directly linked to our goals and therefore to our achievement or success.

Figure 12 below shows the importance / urgency grid. Using this, you can judge your potential activities in terms of how far they are urgent and important.

Urgent and important - Items which are both urgent and important should be done by you as soon as possible. There are two types of task here – those that are unforeseen and those that are known (but haven't been dealt with). These tasks require your specific set of skills / knowledge, lead to achievement of your goals and have a tight deadline. They should therefore demand your first priority.

Urgent and less important - Items with a high urgency rating, but not so important, can be delegated to be done as soon as possible by somebody else. As they are urgent, they need to be actioned; however, the importance is lower and you can therefore identify whether these tasks require your specific skills or can be more effectively delegated. These tasks are obstructing your achievement, they can be time consuming and require a strategy.

Important and less urgent - Items which are important but not necessarily urgent are the ones where you need to be focusing your time as they will lead to the achievement of your goals. This is the area where you should be focusing your time and energy as it will ultimately lead to your success.

Neither important nor urgent - Items which are low in importance and urgency can be delegated to be done later or done by yourself at a low-energy time. They are the mundane, ordinary tasks which will always be around.

Understanding where tasks fit into the grid is the first step to prioritising your workload. Being aware of your team, their strengths, skills and knowledge will help you, as a manager, to delegate effectively and to manage your time better.

However, you need to be aware that prioritising tasks into a grid does not mean they will stay there. Deadlines change and tasks will move.

If you spend too much time focusing on important and urgent tasks, you are not being effective. You will be constantly fire-fighting and not giving the tasks the required attention. You should aim to plan for only 10% of your tasks as important and urgent, 80% of your tasks as being important and not urgent and 10% of your tasks as being neither important nor urgent. Those tasks that are urgent and not important should be delegated. Your personal effectiveness and time management can therefore be seen in a similar grid in figure 13 below:

Delegate to others	Firefighting - 10%
Least effective	Maximum effectiveness

Learning Bite:
Consider your tasks on a daily or weekly basis. List them all and then plot them according to this matrix. Now create a prioritised To Do list.

Many people thrive on lists, relying on them to maintain order in their workload and their daily lives. Lists can be kept on paper, on a smart phone, iPad or laptop. However you choose to keep your list, consider the format.

Take a few minutes at the beginning of each day (or week) or at the end of the previous day, whichever suits you best, to make a list of the activities you need to complete. Begin by prioritising your To Do list, now for each item identify the deadline or timeframe and mark this against the item. As you complete each item, tick them off the list. This will make you feel that you are achieving more and keep you motivated. Never have more than one page of items to do – it is demoralising and you are unlikely to achieve everything. Check your list regularly throughout the day to assess how you are doing.

Lists are not just for To Do items. Keep lists of contacts with you which include details of email address, mobile number, extension number. Keeping it with you means that you can maximise any free time or down time to make a quick phone call or send an email whilst you are waiting for others.

Time Bandits

Whilst you wouldn't let anyone go into your purse or wallet and take out your credit card to use without your permission, you are very likely to let people steal your time. Time bandits are the thieves which rob us of our valuable time. To be effective, we need to consider our time bandits and for each, identify a strategy that will help us reduce the amount of time we lose.

Examples of time bandits include:

- **Paperwork** – aim to handle each piece of paper only once and apply the DAFT technique (Delegate, Action, File or Throw it away).

- **Email** – allocate certain periods of the day to check and respond to email messages, for example first thing, lunchtime and at the end of the afternoon. Don't be distracted by the mail notices popping up on the screen. If you use Outlook or a similar programme, ensure you keep your email to one screen, taking action for each item as it comes in.

- **Procrastination** – putting tasks off only makes them appear larger and more onerous. Stop procrastinating over tasks you don't enjoy and instead promise yourself a reward – for example a coffee or a break once you have finished.

- **Colleagues** who stop to chat idly without good reason – try using the PACE technique (Pause, Ask questions to ascertain how urgent their request is, Choose how you are going to react and Engage and get on with it).

- **Lateness** – if someone is late for an appointment with you, stress that you only have until the scheduled finish time and finish the appointment on time.

- **Meetings** – poorly managed and badly run meetings cause delays. For meetings you manage, ensure you prepare appropriately, start on time and stick to the agenda.

- **Telephone calls** – allocate periods of the day for returning and making telephone calls. Ensure you have all required information to hand and always be prepared to leave a message. If you are calling someone who you know likes to chat, call just before lunchtime or at the end of the day when they are less inclined to talk. Use voicemail effectively to allow yourself quiet time to concentrate on work or projects.

- **Working environment** – consider how you can more effectively organise your working environment. Use wall planners to record notable dates and deadlines. Adopt different colour codes for different events – holidays, different types of meetings, deadlines – to provide a visual, at-a-glance view of what is going on. Maintain a clear desk policy, putting everything away at night – it clears the mind for the next morning and helps to maintain confidentiality of information.

These are just a few of the time bandits you will find to hamper your time management. Each individual and each role will be different and you will need to consider your own strategies for maximising your time.

Learning Bite:
Consider your own time bandits. What strategies can you employ to maximise your time effectiveness?

Delegation

Delegation is about empowering other people to perform tasks. It is about maximising people's skills at the appropriate level within an organisation. For example, taking the minutes of a meeting is neither a cost-effective or efficient use of time for a senior manager when the task can be done and at a lower cost by a secretary. So delegation is about ensuring that work tasks are assigned to the lowest level to maximise productivity within a department or an organisation.

Delegation is simply the assignment of a specific task or set of tasks to another person or team and, in turn, their commitment to complete the task. It is one of the most important skills demonstrated by successful managers and yet it is frequently neglected by managers. Effective managers will invest time in planning work delegation and organising their resources to achieve their targets in the most effective and efficient way.

To delegate appropriately, you need to understand the skills profile of your team. This means completing an analysis of people's knowledge, skills, experience, workload level and development needs. Delegation is a powerful way of motivating staff through empowerment and trust.

So why don't managers delegate more? There are several reasons for this.

One reason is trust or lack of trust. Managers lack the confidence in their staff that the task will be done to the highest standard. The manager is accountable for maintaining established standards and there is the niggling fear that delegated work won't meet the same standard. Delegation is like taking out your credit card and passing it to someone else to go shopping. It requires trust.

Time is another reason. It is often quicker to carry out the task yourself than to take the time to explain to someone else what needs to be done and how. This is a poor excuse as taking the time to show someone how something needs to be done is more profitable in the longer term as the other person will be able to help out in future and you are motivating that member of staff

Perception is also a reason. Some managers don't want to be perceived to be delegating tasks to their staff which they could do themselves as they feel they will be accused of 'sloping shoulders'.

Benefits of Delegation

There are many benefits of delegation – applicable to individuals, teams, managers and organisations:

Individual / team	Manager	Organisation
Recognition of skills / knowledge and experience Feeling empowered and valued Sense of trust Opportunity to enhance existing skills and to develop new skills Contributes to sense of achievement and job satisfaction Develops team in terms of skills and morale Improved motivation levels	Improves level of trust with team Develops communication between staff Achieves goals that require team effort and co-operation More effective time management Frees up time to focus on other activities ie service improvements Motivated and empowered staff are easier to manage	Develops leadership skills within the organisation Makes most effective use of staff skills and knowledge Saves money for the organisation ensuring tasks are assigned to right person at the right level Increases overall productivity and efficiency by making best use of resources

Delegation requires empowering staff and giving them responsibility for a task. As a delegating manager, you should focus on results rather than the method of completing the task as this may be seen as a lack of trust.

There are three ways of delegating:

- **By task** – the simplest and most common form of delegating. This involves assigning a simple task to another person either as a single one-off event or on a continuous basis.

- **By project** – another popular way of delegating is to assign a group of tasks or project to one or more people. This may include the organisation of an event, carrying out a study, audit or survey or the implementation of a change.

- **By function** – this is typically done within the organisational structure of a company, although it will also occur within teams and departments. For example, a managing director may allocate all responsibility for finance to a finance manager or a department manager may delegate all responsibility for a budget to a team member.

There are certain tasks which should not be delegated and these include those associated with the specific skillset of the role. Managers should not delegate 'people management' tasks like appraisal, managing performance, recruitment or discipline (unless it is delegated within the agreed hierarchical structure). Neither should a manager delegate tasks that require their specific expertise.

Most managers will begin by delegating by task as this is the simplest and most common form of delegation.

Learning Bite:
Consider your current workload. What are three tasks that you already delegate? Now consider another three tasks that you could delegate. Why aren't you currently delegating these tasks?

When delegating a project or more complex tasks, there are four stages to follow as can be seen in figure 14 below:

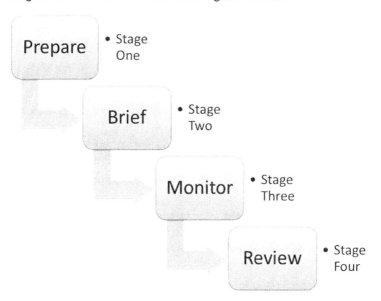

Stage one - the first task is to decide what can and cannot be delegated and then consider the most appropriate person in the team for the delegation. We tend to delegate to strength by selecting the person with the right skills and attitude. To really be effective as a manager, you need to consider delegating to weakness to develop staff. Certain other factors need to be considered too:

- What resources and equipment will be needed?

- What skills are needed? Think technical skills, interpersonal skills and problem-solving skills.

- What is the timeframe and time commitment?

- What is the current workload and commitment (including holiday) of your team?

Once you have identified a staff member for the delegation, you need to consider your own style of delegation. This will involve an understanding of the individual and the task. For someone you are developing you will need a more hands-on, coaching style of management to encourage and guide them. For someone who is experienced, you need a more delegating style of management to allow them to get on with the task without too much interference.

Stage two – brief the member of staff. This means outlining the task to them in terms of:

- Background to the task and the delegation

- Outcome or objectives from the task including overview of resources and support available to the individual

- Authority – providing appropriate level of authority for the staff member to act on your behalf. This may also involve briefing other people about the level of authority for the individual

- Timeframe or deadline for the task

- Support – outline the level of support you are happy to provide and ensure the individual is happy with this

Stage three – monitor the delegation. Here you need to consider your own style as a manager. Delegators frequently find it difficult to leave staff to simply get on with the task in their own way which causes problems and frustration for the individual. Monitor the delegation through pre-agreed review discussions, regular email updates, reports or meetings – whatever is appropriate for the task, the individual and agreed during the briefing stage.

Stage four – review the task. Once the task or project has been completed, review the results and the method. Meet with the employee for a review and listen to how they feel things went. Consider what has gone well and where improvements could have been made. Look at what the individual has learned from the experience. Give feedback and praise, showing that you value their work and avoid criticising or attributing blame.

Tips for Effective Delegation

- Understand your staff profile

- Develop trust with your staff

- Focus on results – and avoid focusing on the method

- Delegate to those who can develop their skills

- Always delegate to the lowest possible level

- Brief employees appropriately

- Provide feedback and praise at the end

People Management

The human resources are the most valuable asset of an organisation. Effective managers are continually observing their staff to see how they behave and perform at work both with clients and with other team members. This observation is a way of gathering information to facilitate the process of developing staff in their roles through consideration of their skills, knowledge and competencies and the ways in which they effectively fulfil their responsibilities and provide a quality service.

This informal observation should be viewed as integral to the formal processes of appraisal, supervision, feedback, mentoring, objective setting and training needs analysis. Combined they provide a way of developing staff in their roles, remembering that each employee is an individual with different strengths and development areas.

In this section we will look at various aspects of people management – the most rewarding and also arguably the most difficult part of management.

Team Dynamics

People are individuals – bringing people together creates teams. Therefore the combination of each team is unique with its own dynamics.

Let's start at the beginning by considering what constitutes a team and what makes a group.

A group is a random selection of people who have something in common. This may be through a shared interest, common goals, membership or the same place at the same time. Groups may be large and extensive, for example cultural groups. They may be small and compact, for example a queue for a bus. However, size is largely irrelevant. A group will differ from a team in several ways:

- Relationships tend to be formal, cautious and selective – we're unlikely to talk to other people waiting for the train and, if we choose to do so, we are selective about who we talk to and limit the topics of conversation.

- There is no hierarchy or structure to a group, therefore there is no leader – although in certain groups as they begin to bond, a leader may develop, for example during riots and strike action.

- Individuals within a group have their own goals and objectives – there are no common or shared goals, although there will be a shared interest, for example a football crowd or theatre audience.

- Individuals have their own roles and work independently. There is little or no co-operation between individuals in a group and roles are neither collaborative nor co-dependent

A team has been described by Katzenbach and Smith[xxviii] as "a small number of people with complementary skills who are committed to a common purpose, performance goals and approach for which they hold themselves mutually accountable".

Various studies conducted into team dynamics show that the size of a team does matter although it depends on the role of the team. Teams vary in size from two individuals to around twenty. The optimum number is seen to between five and seven although opinion differs widely. Teams differ from groups in a number of ways:

- A team will have some structure, hierarchy (although typically flat) and a leader.

- There will be agreed decision making processes in place so that all team members are involved in making decisions.

- Team members work interdependently. They rely on each other and their skills should complement each other to provide a cohesive team-working approach. There is collaboration and co-operation in place.

- Relationships tend to be more informal, trusting and supportive and these will develop the longer the team is together.

- Although each individual team member will have personal goals, there will also be team objectives, which are usually decided together, and a team approach and process established together.

There are different sorts of team depending on the organisation and the work involved. These will fall into three categories:

- **Management teams** – usually senior managers or managers of a similar level who are responsible for different functions in a company. They will come together to discuss issues and opportunities, to reach a common understanding and make decisions about the operational side of a company.

- **Project teams** – may also be known as task force team, these are teams which have been established with a specific purpose or objective. The lifespan of a project team is usually identified at the beginning and will be for a specific length of time. These teams will consist of people with different (relevant) areas of expertise operating at a similar level. Once objectives have been completed, the team will disband. Quality Improvement Teams (QITs) will have similar characteristics.

- **Departmental teams** – the type of team most commonly found, these will be people working together to deliver a service or a product. Most organisational activity will be conducted through departmental teams, ie learning and development, ward nursing and printing departments.

Most organisations promote team working through the organisational structure and culture recognising that the benefits of team working typically result in more motivated staff. However, the culture is an important aspect of team working. An organisation that encourages self-development, well-being and employee support is promoting the effectiveness of positive team working.

Benefits of Team Working

The benefits of team working for individuals and organisations are many and varied and include:

- Increased creativity which encourages more effective problem solving. In a trusting team climate, members feel encouraged to put forward ideas for improvement and will bounce ideas off each other.

- Improved communication skills as relationships tend to develop into more informal, trusting and supportive relationships.

- Team synergy or team spirit is perhaps the biggest benefit of team organisations. People working within teams develop a team spirit between them which encourages responsibility and improves job satisfaction.

- Most people find it less isolating and more motivating to work in a team than alone.

- Team working encourages people to develop their own and other team members' skills, knowledge, confidence and experience.

- There is a greater co-ordination of tasks, shared workload and less disruption when team members are away and increased productivity with more effective use of time.

- Team members feel more supported, both emotionally and in terms of workload support than when they are working in isolation.

- There is increased opportunity for sharing and allocating resources between a team.

Problems of Team Working

Whilst the benefits of team working are seen to outweigh the disadvantages, the manager needs to be aware of potential problems. Alert to these, the manager can make early observations and take action to prevent damage to the team and team working process.

Problems include:

- As teams work well together and informal relationships develop, so does the tendency to talk. For this reason, things may take longer on occasion, particularly when there is a lot of discussion over the best way to tackle tasks.

- Teams need time to grow together and most working environments do not allow the time for people to establish team working processes for the teams to become as effective as possible.

- Tolerance and compromise is required in any working environment, particularly with team working. Where this doesn't exist, there will be problems both in the team working pattern and in the productivity of the team.

- Blaming each other can result in poor team working. This is usually attributed to team members who are unwilling to take responsibility within a team and therefore are not fully contributing to the team.

- Unbalanced participation from team members – this may be where some team members are quick to avoid tasks or responsibilities; equally it could be where dominant members shoulder too much responsibility.

- Some team members may 'opt out' – this could be because of poor working relationships within the team, intimidation from other team members, reluctance to participate in the team process or an over-riding desire to focus on personal objectives rather than team objectives.

- Groupthink may evolve where teams develop such cohesive views within the team that they fail to challenge each other's views and adopt a team approach. It was identified as a problem in political arenas through the work of Janis[xxix].

- In some teams, individuals become so much a part of the team that they tend to lose their individuality leading to loss of confidence when working away from the team environment.

However, it is generally considered that team working leads to more productive results.

Lifecycle of a Team

Whilst it is generally acknowledged that teams will begin to develop out of groups because of a shared identity and feeling of belonging, there is no guarantee that these will develop fully into effective teams. This takes time, effort, tolerance and compromise. It requires giving and taking, sharing responsibility, showing respect for each other, developing trust and an ability to work interdependently as well as independently as required.

Bruce Tuckman[xxx] developed the idea of the lifecycle of a group in 1965 identifying four stages of team dynamics. He further expanded on this work in 1977 by adding a fifth stage, acknowledging the feelings people feel when a team is disbanded.

Figure 15 below shows Tuckman's lifecycle of a team:

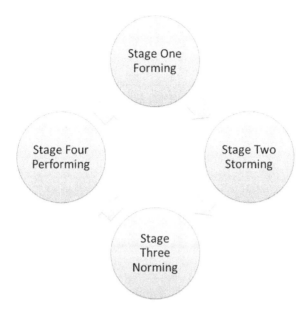

The four different stages can be characterized as:

Stage One – Forming – this is the time when the group are coming together and the team is 'forming'. Behaviour is driven by a need to be accepted and to fit in. Relationships tend to be formal and selective whilst people get to know each other a little and find out more about what their roles will be. Conflict and problems are avoided as people gather information about the other members, the team objectives and tasks. Team members are not working together yet, but independently. It is an important stage of the team formation as it allows people an opportunity to find out more about each other, begin to develop relationships and it permits the manager to observe and find out about the individuals.

Stage Two – Storming – this is the second stage of the team and the most difficult phase for both team members and the manager. People are beginning to feel more established in the team and begin to compete with each other for preferred roles, tasks and ideas. Behaviour becomes more confrontational as members begin to challenge each other's ideas and viewpoints. Whilst it is an essential time for a team, it is also a difficult and destructive time which needs careful management. Some teams will never move beyond the storming stage for various reasons.

Stage Three - Norming – as the team move toward the third stage, they are beginning to settle down. Members are assuming roles in which they are comfortable. Objectives have been agreed and compromises reached for the sake of the team's productivity. Processes are being put in place to establish a more effective working pattern and team members are beginning to form supportive, trusting relationships with each other which encourages team cohesion and co-operation. The team is beginning to work effectively as a team.

Stage Four – Performing – the final stage of the team process where all team members are working well. There is little conflict and problems. Tasks are approached systematically and tackled quickly and effectively. Team customs become part of the working pattern. Members are aware of each other's skills and knowledge and work effectively together.

It takes time for teams to grow together and it may take several months or even a couple of years to reach the 'performing' stage of the lifecycle. For many teams, they will never reach this stage. In today's every-changing working environments with people moving roles frequently, the challenges of reaching the norming and performing stages are even greater. Even where teams reach the performing stage, there is no guarantee they will stay there. Team dynamics mean that as people leave and move onto other roles, the team itself may revert to the norming or even the storming phase.

Learning Bite:
Consider your team – what stage of the lifecycle are you at currently? How can you identify the stage? What actions can you take to move the team forward to the next stage?

For the manager, this can be the key to the most appropriate management style for the team. Thinking back to the situational leadership style we examined in chapter 3, we can see some correlation between the different management styles and each stage of Tuckman's Team Lifecycle. Figure 16 below shows the most appropriate style for each stage:

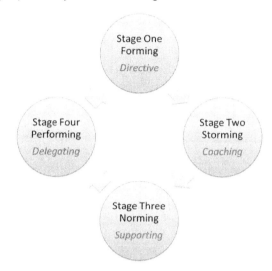

During the first stage, the manager needs to take control of the team and use a more directive style. As the team move into the storming phase, a coaching style will help to both direct and support team members during a time of conflict and difficulties. A supporting style of management is most suited to stage three where the team are settling into roles and working well. Finally the manager can afford to take a more delegating style working alongside the team as they become more effective in the final performing stage.

In 1977, Bruce Tuckman added a fifth stage to his team lifecycle. He called this the 'adjourning' or 'mourning' stage. During this stage the team would be dissolved and people would begin moving onto other roles in other teams. For some, this stage would be straightforward whilst for others this dissolution would be difficult and stressful. Some people may go through a feeling of loss for the team synergy and team spirit and would need to adjust to this before fully integrating in a new team.

The success of a team will depend on actively moving through to the norming and performing stages; however, other variables will also contribute. These include the team climate which considers the impact of the leader or manager on the team and the degree to which the leader is accepted and respected by the team members. This will also be influenced by the power and authority exerted by the leader over the team and to what degree the manager is able to 'manage' the team through personal power and positional authority. A second variable will be the tasks themselves and the extent to which the team understand, value and work towards the objectives. A third variable will be the organisational culture which will influence the team philosophy.

Team Direction

For teams to grow, they need to have a goal, an objective or a mission. A team's objectives will be derived from corporate objectives which are in turn fed down through the hierarchy. These corporate objectives may vary from year to year but will revolve around the organisational vision and mission statement.

Figure 17 shows the different levels of objectives and the link between team objectives and departmental and corporate objectives:

Organisation	Division	Team
Mission Statement	Mission for Division	Team Purpose
Corporate Objectives	Divisional Objectives	Team Objectives

A team with clear objectives has something to aim for, something to work towards and something to achieve. Goals provide the shared purpose and help to establish cohesion.

Some teams will have objectives set for them – these will come from above and be part of the reason for the team formation, for example a project team may have a SMART objective:

> "to implement the new XXX software package and ensure all users are trained and able to use the system by 31st October 20xx"

The team members know that they have a goal to achieve (implementation), a standard to aim for (users' ability in system use) and a specific timeframe (deadline). This will allow them to assess the skills required, the resources needed and to plan the work amongst the team members accordingly.

Other teams may decide objectives for themselves. Often departmental teams will hold an 'away day' at the beginning of a financial year to assess the priorities for their department, to set objectives and to identify standards. Where the team players are involved in deciding the goals, the commitment to achieve is higher. This is an important part of the team building process ensuring shared responsibility for results.

Team Roles

For a team to function effectively, the members need to bring complementary skills and ability to fulfil certain roles within a team. The roles will depend on the objectives and function of the team. However, certain roles will always be required.

The most popular work on team roles has been researched and profiled by Dr Meredith Belbin[xxxi]. Commissioned by Henley Management College in the 1970s, Belbin researched why some management teams functioned better than others by examining the relationship between the input and output of different teams and conducting psychometric tests to identify personality traits in team members. His conclusions after a number of years led Belbin to identify eight key roles needed within a team. He later added a ninth role. Some of the initial names given for these roles have been changed, so different names are included below.

These roles were:

Chair or Coordinator
This was one of two managers identified. The chair focuses on people and achieving results through the best use of its members understanding where their strengths and weaknesses lie. The chair is usually confident in their own ability, mature and willing to delegate and trust team members to develop and build the team. They have a broad outlook and generally bring out the best in their people. On the downside their management style may conflict with the organisational culture if achievement and objective are paramount.

Shaper
This is the second manager. The shaper focuses on objectives and

priorities. They are self-motivated, driven by targets, deadlines and objectives. Shapers like to generate action and impose direction on a team. They are not keen on lengthy discussion preferring to reach quick decisions. They are typically assertive but may come across as aggressive and pushy. Their style may also conflict with the organisational culture where this is more people-centred.

Plant

The plant is the creative and innovative member of a team who will thrive in generating ideas and coming up with solutions for problems. They are usually lateral thinkers with an imaginative disposition. They are unorthodox and intelligent. The plant's strength lies in generating solutions, not necessarily in seeing them through. They can appear quite eccentric and sensitive to criticism.

Monitor Evaluator

This is the policeman or judge in the team. Their strengths lie in analysing and evaluating situations. They provide very shrewd judgement and like to fully evaluate before reaching a decision. They lack enthusiasm and may come across as blunt and critical.

Resource Investigator

This is the PR person in the team who frequently prefers to work outside the team on their behalf rather than within the team. They are enthusiastic, good communicators and outgoing. Their strengths lie in developing ideas, exploring opportunities and building relationships and contacts outside the team. On the downside their enthusiasm fades and they need constant stimulus to remain motivated.

Implementer or

These are the backbone of every team

Company Worker	as they focus on getting on with tasks and hard work. They are reliable, self-sufficient and work in a systematic, methodical way. They are efficient and self-disciplined. However, they can appear to lack spontaneity and are often quite inflexible in their approach.
Completer Finisher	The completer finisher is the team perfectionist and will focus on quality. They pay great attention to detail and are highly accurate. They foster a sense of urgency and are unlikely to start something if they are unable to finish. They work to a high standard and do not like to delegate to others. They may come across as being pernickety and fussy.
Team worker or *Team Builder*	These people are needed in every team to bring people together. Their strengths lie in supporting others by building on suggestions, organising team gatherings, improving communications and generating a team spirit and synergy. Team workers are sociable, flexible, perceptive and concerned with others. On the downside they are indecisive in crunch situations and don't like friction in the team.
Specialist	These are people who are highly specialist in a particular area and whose focus centres around their specialist topic. They have very high standards, maintain professionalism and take great pride in their subject. Whilst useful to teams with a specialist focus, they are single-minded and not interested in other people or their areas of expertise .

Belbin identified that there are likely to be two or three roles in which each individual operates most effectively. These are the roles they will choose for themselves and where they have most to contribute to the team. Each person will also have two or three roles where they score lowest and, if placed in these roles, they will not be able to contribute as well to a team and may become demotivated. The middle three roles are areas where they can operate if they need to. Whilst some roles require a distinct personality set (for example plant or specialist) most of us can function in any of the roles if required. A team will work best with a balance of roles and only one sort of leader. Where there is a distinct lack of roles, the team manager will need to counterbalance this.

Learning Bite:
Consider your own strengths and weaknesses when working in a team. Where do you believe your preferences lie? In which roles are you likely to be least effective?

To help us identify the different requirements of teams, let us look at different types of teams and who would be required.

A '**brainstorming**' session would be best led by a Coordinator manager who would bring out the best in people, encouraging input and promoting ideas. At least one Plant would be needed to come up with ideas and stimulate creative thinking from other participants. Team Builders will help to bring the team together and promote goodwill. A Specialist may be required depending on the topic.

A '**decision making**' session would be best led by a Shaper who can quickly lead the team towards the objective. A Monitor Evaluator would be beneficial in analysing and evaluating different options and a Resource Investigator for developing ideas further. Team Builders would also help although are not essential at this stage.

A '**project implementation**' team would require a Shaper as a manager to focus on outcome. Implementers are needed to get the work done and Completer Finishers to ensure high quality. Again Team Builders may be beneficial.

Developing Individuals

The human resources are the most valuable asset of an organisation.

Effective managers are continually observing their staff to see how they behave and perform at work both with clients and with other team members. This observation is a way of gathering information to facilitate the process of developing staff in the skills, knowledge and competencies they need to effectively fulfil their responsibilities and provide a quality service.

This informal observation should be viewed as integral to the formal processes of appraisal, supervision, feedback, mentoring, objective setting and training needs analysis. Combined they provide a way of developing staff in their roles, remembering that each employee is an individual with different strengths and development areas.

In looking at developing individuals it is difficult to identify the most appropriate starting point. However, generally development needs will be identified as part of the performance management process.

Performance Management

Performance management is the review process to evaluate how employees are performing against objectives previously agreed between manager and employee. This is typically a process that is:

- Formal

- Annual

- Documented

- Against job objectives, KPIs, job description or individual achievements

Performance management is essential so that we can monitor how individuals are doing, how teams are performing and how the organisation is doing. We need to manage individual and team performance for a variety of reasons which include making decisions about rewards and incentives, achieving improvements in performance, increasing productivity by continually monitoring performance and providing timely feedback to staff to identify potential and develop the individual. Appraisal is an opportunity to consider an individual's potential and look at ways of developing them. For some organisations, appraisal and performance management will include feeding succession planning systems within the company and enabling the organisation to make decisions regarding promotion and pay.

It is important to identify poor performance and deal with problems as quickly as possible for both the individual and the team. Performance management is a way of formally showing staff that you value their contribution to the team, that you recognise their potential, to show people where they fit in to a team and generate a sense of belonging within the company, thereby motivating staff.

There are a number of tools available that will help the manager in managing performance. These include:

- **Job description** – this gives an overview of the role and is used in the recruitment process as well as in managing performance. It will usually provide the main objective or purpose of the role, the scope, the main tasks and responsibilities of the post holder, the skills required and level of accountability.

- **Work / service / business objectives** – these are the tasks or objectives to be undertaken over a set period of time and should include some form of measurement. It may simply be a list of outcomes required from the role over a certain period of time. Some organisations may have Key Performance indicators (KPIs) which are used for this purpose.

- **Person specification** – this is used more typically when people are applying for particular roles and looks at the experience, qualifications, competencies and personal attributes required. These are frequently categorised under 'essential' and 'desirable'. However, these can be used as a useful base for looking at staff development in post.

Appraisals

Appraisals began to grow in popularity in the mid-1990s with the purpose of improving performance, identifying training needs and encouraging a dialogue between the manager and individuals.

Appraisal is an opportunity to 'praise' staff, give them feedback and show they are valued. Most organisations will have their own framework and documentation for appraisal which will generally include reviewing work objectives or KPIs, consideration of development needs, setting future work and personal development objectives. It will include a review of any statutory or mandatory training requirements for the role or organisation. Unfortunately for many managers, appraisals are seen as a tick-box exercise that has to be carried out on an annual basis with each member of staff.

There are different types of appraisal, all of which bring benefit to the workplace:

- **Informal -** usually held at regular intervals in between formal appraisals or on an ad hoc basis. An opportunity to chat informally about issues and look at ways of solving problems or resolving conflict without resorting to formal channels. Informal appraisals are a way of intercepting issues before they become problems and addressing behaviours or attitudes before they get out of hand.

- **Formal** – these are the formal appraisals or reviews held annually or six-monthly depending on the organisation's culture and policies. A formal review requires preparation by the manager and employee and will usually take between one and two hours. It will usually be structured and focused. It will normally be documented and copies held on the employee's personal file.

- **Upward Appraisal** – this is where a more junior person is asked to appraise a more senior person. It is quite common in American companies and can either stand alone or form part of a 360 degree appraisal system. Typically employees are asked to complete a questionnaire on their manager which may include communication, motivation, setting realistic objectives, effective planning etc. The combined scores are then given to the manager.

- **360 Degree Appraisal** – this is becoming the norm in many companies who appreciate that feedback from different sources is more valuable than a simple manager-employee assessment. Most 360 degree appraisals depend on at least four individual inputs – typically, the employee, the manager and at least two peers, colleagues or customers, depending on the job being done. The inputs follow a set format and are combined. Often it is the responsibility of the employee to gather and collate feedback which is then given to the manager in advance of the actual review.

Role of the Manager in Appraisal

Each manager is responsible for the informal and formal appraisal of staff in their team and this will include the following duties:

- Set objectives
- Monitor performance against business objectives

- Monitor performance against personal development objectives
- Review regularly, consistently and confidentially
- Advise, guide and coach staff in developing skills
- Provide useful and timely feedback
- Manage underperformance

Formal appraisals should be conducted in a private, quiet place (usually the manager's office) and are likely to take between one and two hours. Staff should be given notice of their appraisal – a week or two is normal – and advised of any preparation they are required to do. Most managers and staff will need to prepare for the appraisal by considering performance over the past year against objectives and identifying future development needs. Useful questions for the manager to consider in preparing for an appraisal may include:

- What has been the greatest achievement over the past year (for staff member)?

- What have they done particularly well?

- How have they participated as a team member in helping others?

- What has timekeeping, absence and punctuality been like?

- Have there been any incidents that have been particularly positive (or negative)?

- Has there been feedback from other people which may include customers, peers, other managers?

- How have problems been dealt with?

- What development have they had? And how have they applied this to their role?

- Are there changes to the role, to the team or to the organisation coming up which may have an impact?

- How is the role likely to develop?

- How does the individual need to develop?

Where there are problems which need to be highlighted, you may want to gather some supporting information to show that the feedback is objective and not your subjective view. Supporting information may include written evidence of poor work, feedback from others, customer complaints or incidents that have happened. You will need specific examples for the feedback to be meaningful.

During the appraisal, the balance of talking should be approximately 70:30 – the manager being 30% and the staff member being 70%. There should be a clear structure which begins with ice-breaker questions to develop rapport, leading into a review of performance against current objectives, setting future work objectives for the next period, review of development undertaken and assessment of knowledge and skills in post with future development requirements identified. An appraisal should conclude with a document that will detail the review discussion, future work objectives and future development objectives. This is usually signed by both manager and individual, both will retain copies.

Learning Bite:
Consider appraisals you have had in the past. How meaningful were they? Did you come away feeling motivated and inspired? Or did you come away feeling it has been a tick-box exercise and a waste of an hour?

How can you develop your appraisal technique to make the appraisal more meaningful for your staff?

Developing staff is one of the most rewarding parts of a manager's role and is certainly one of the most important in terms of maintaining a motivated and productive workforce. Whilst staff development will naturally fall out of the appraisal process, it is useful to have a framework within which to structure the discussion with the individual to look at the best way of developing staff needs. This is particularly true when you have new staff working for you whom you may not know very well. A tool like DIFSWOT can frame this:

- **D** – difficult or demanding. Identify the challenging aspects of the role, the more difficult responsibilities. Consider the reasons why these are particularly difficult. Can it be due to processes, resources or the individual's own development needs?

- **I** – interesting or important. Identify the most interesting or important aspects of the role. What are the reasons for this? Is it due to the particular aspect or because the staff member has a particular skill in this area?

- **F** – frequent or time-consuming. Identify the most frequent tasks or activities, or the ones which are most time-consuming. Are individuals spending their time on the most important activities or the ones where they are most confident?

- **S** – strengths. Identify the individual's strengths and how these impact on their role, their performance and the team.

- **W** – weaknesses. Consider the individual's weaker areas which need to be addressed.

- – opportunities. Consider what opportunities there are to develop the individual taking into account the learning goals, the learning need and the learning styles as well as availability, funding and other constraints.

- **T** – threats. Identify the aspects of the role which an individual doesn't enjoy and consider the reasons. Are these because of a development need or because of a lack of interest or job fatigue?

Although this model is a useful tool in considering employee development, you may choose to change the order or eliminate certain aspects.

Once a DIFSWOT has been completed, you should consider the individual's strengths and weaknesses in light of the difficult and important tasks known. From here you will be able to identify any gaps around which to focus and direct development and training.

A 'learning gap' is looking at the difference between where an individual is and where an individual needs to be to deliver the best service.

Consider Figure 18 below:

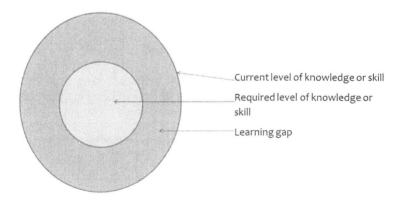

Current level of knowledge or skill

Required level of knowledge or skill

Learning gap

When the learning gap has been identified, the next stage is to identify the most appropriate way to develop staff. Whilst most people will consider that formal training is the most common way of developing staff, there are many different ways to develop staff which may be far more effective for the individual.

Learning Styles

Just as each of your staff members requires a different style of management, so each may require a different style of development. Learning styles help us to understand our preferred ways of learning. Choosing the most effective learning methods and activities for each individual will maximise the impact of the development. There are a plethora of learning styles available. The most popular one is probably Honey & Mumford's[xxxii] learning styles. Their Learning Styles Questionnaire (LSQ) was based on Kolb's learning cycle and they identified four dominant learning styles for which most people will have a preference for one or two:

- **Activist** - Involve themselves fully and without bias in new experiences, happy to be dominated by immediate experiences. They are open-minded and generally enthusiastic with a philosophy of "I'll try anything once". This may mean they will act first and consider the consequences later. Their preferred learning activities will involve other people, challenges, problem solving, role-play, brainstorming in small groups and team activities.

- **Reflector** – Generally quieter, they prefer to stand back, observe others and ponder experiences. Generally quite cautious, they prefer to understand a situation before adding their views and will frequently take a back seat in training sessions. Their preferred learning activities centre around reflection, quiet activities, reading, listening to others. For reflectors, the learning comes later once they have had a chance to assimilate their learning experience and reflect.

- **Theorist** – Logical thinkers who prefer to approach situations in a sequential, logical way allowing them to analyse, evaluate and reach their own conclusions. They are often perfectionists who like to ask 'why?' and seek to analyse and synthesise. They are keen on principles, theories, systems thinking, rationale and logic. Their preferred learning activities centre around research, case studies and lectures.

- **Pragmatist** – Practical learners keen on trying out ideas to see if they work in practice so long as there is a link to the task. They are like an activist with a mission as they will positively search out new ideas and are keen to apply to practice, if they can identify a link. Their preferred learning activities include coaching, feedback and practical-based activities.

Learning Point:

Considering the above learning styles, which do you believe is your preferred style? How do you learn best?

Another popular learning styles inventory is the VAK Learning styles. This is amongst the most popular as it is appropriate for all learners from young children through to adult learners. Several variations of VAK may be found including VARK and VACT – all variations on the original concepts which were developed during the 1920s and 1930s by psychologists and teaching specialists. The principles and benefits of VAK extend to all different types of learning and development.

Based on principles of Neuro-Linguistic Programming (NLP), VAK is derived from three of the five senses – the three through which we typically absorb information and communicate:

V – Visual - seeing and reading

A – Auditory – hearing and listening

K - Kinaesthetic – touching and doing

To find out your preference, take the short self-assessment:

VAK Learning Styles Questionnaire

For each of the following statements, circle the option that most appeals to you. You should try to answer every one and only select one option for each.

Question	Option A	Option B	Option C
In my free time, I would prefer to:	Read a good book	Listen to music	Go to the gym
If I go out in the evening I would choose	Cinema or theatre	Music concert	Dancing
When I'm with other people, I like to	Watch others	Listen to others	Join in
If someone is explaining something to me	I like pictures or diagrams	I prefer them to explain in words	I like to have a go as they talk
If I have a problem to sort out, I prefer to	Draw a mind-map or make a list	Talk through it with a friend	Try different solutions
When I'm trying to find my way	I always use a map	I like sat nav to tell me	I'll just take the route that feels right
I frequently form opinions of other people by	Watching their body language	Listening to their voice	Gut feel of what they are like
I am most likely to say	I see what you mean	I hear what you say	That feels right to me
When I'm at home, I like to have	Lots of photos and pictures	The radio or music on	A home that feels comfortable
When I have a	Read the	Ask someone	Have a go

new piece of equipment, I always	manual	else to explain	
When I think of people in my past, I	Remember faces clearly	Remember names, but not faces	Remember how I felt towards them
If someone is testing my knowledge, I would prefer	A written test	An oral test	Demonstration
When I meet someone new, I form an opinion by	What they look like	What their voice sounds like	How they shake hands
When I'm cooking a new dish, I like to	Follow a recipe	Ask a friend for instructions	Have a go and taste as I go
If I'm explaining something or teaching someone, I tend to	Give them written instructions	Tell them how to do it	Get them to have a go
If I have a complaint, I will usually	Write a letter	Make a telephone call	Go into the shop
When I'm planning a holiday, I like to	Look up places on the internet or in brochures	Ask other people for recommendations	Imagine what places are like
When I'm listening to music at home, I like to	Sing along	Listen to the words and music	Dance along to the rhythm
TOTALS			

Now add up your scores to find your preference:

a. Visual   =
b. Auditory   =
c. Kinaesthetic   =

Your highest score will be your preference

© Desiree Cox, 2010

Visual learning style involves the use of seen or observed things, including pictures, diagrams, demonstrations, displays, hand-outs, films, and flipcharts. Visual people learn through reading to themselves, watching films or presentations. Visual learners will remember pictures or written words.

Auditory learning style involves the transfer of information through listening to the spoken word, of self or others, of sounds and noises. Auditory learners enjoy listening to others reading aloud, the radio or CDs. They distinguish tone, language and expression and remember heard detail rather than visual.

Kinaesthetic learning involves physical experience - touching, feeling, holding, doing and practical hands-on experiences. Kinaesthetic learners find it difficult to concentrate for long periods of time. They learn best through doing and trying things out. They become frustrated listening without the facility to actually try and do for themselves. They are experiential learners.

Learning Bite:
Consider your preferred learning style and identify activities best suited to you. Are these the ones you enjoy most? Can you give examples of development activity you have undertaken which have been beneficial and others which have not been useful?

Once the preferred learning style has been identified, the next stage is to consider the most appropriate learning activity taking account of the learning need, the learning style and the learning options available considering time, funding and the individual's own requirements.

Learning activities may include some or all of the following:

- **Formal training courses** – these will typically be classroom-based and include a variety of learners either within one organisation or from different organisations.

- **Delegation** – delegating tasks or projects appropriately to empower staff and develop their level of knowledge, skill or experience.

- **E-learning** – increasingly popular with staff as it provides a low-cost training option which is flexible enough for staff to do at different times which are best suited to their work commitments.

- **Coaching** – one-to-one coaching with individuals focusing on particular areas of development. This is explored in further detail later in this book.

- **Peer support** – buddying individuals to develop individuals. This works well with new staff and provides development for the more experienced peer in terms of communication skills.

- **Mentoring** – different people place different interpretations on mentoring which may include peer support, new staff buddying and role-modelling. Mentoring will also be explored in further detail later in this book.

- **Self-directed study** – may include a variety of activities which the individual will choose and may incorporate reading, research, reviewing articles or processes

- **Case studies** – discussion of previous cases in small groups to identify what had been done, how well and what could be learned.

- **Action learning** – working with a group of others to share problems, views and ideas. This works best with a mix of people from different areas who can offer different perspectives but relies on individuals taking the learning away from the set.

- **Role play or simulation** – whilst not popular with learners this is one of the most effective ways of practising and developing skills.

- **Presentations / lectures** – given by experts in an area, these usually offer short capsule learning.

There are many ways to develop staff and the key is identifying the most suitable activity for the individual given any constraints within the organisation.

Development objectives

The next stage is to develop SMART objectives that will both motivate the staff member and provide the focus of development over the required timeframe. Another mnemonic to remember in setting objectives for personal development is AIM:

A – attitude. Consider the staff member's attitude towards development. Identify the best ways to motivate them by linking development activities to their learning style and to their own individual aspirations.

I – interest. Consider the interests of the individual and the organisation. If the individual is not interested in the development and motivation is low, it is unlikely to be of any benefit to the organisation. Focusing activities to the individual's interests will stimulate the motivation essential in effective development and lead to a more-motivated and productive staff member

M – measurement. Without measurement of the effect, there can be no indication of success or achievement. Individuals need clear, measured goals to ensure they know what needs to be achieved and within what timeframe. This encourages learning and inspires effective application to the workplace.

Development objectives should be clear, concise and realistic. Verbs like improve, understand or develop are best avoided as they are seen as woolly, difficult to quantify and to measure. Good practice suggests that a maximum of three personal development objectives are sufficient – any more than that and the staff member may feel demotivated with the amount of development and improvement required.

In considering development objectives, thought should be given to the application of the newly learned skill to the workplace and the provision of sufficient opportunity to consolidate the learning. An understanding of how people apply their learning is useful. One of the best models for this is the pyramid of learning that was developed by Anderson & Krathwohl[xxxiii] based on Bloom's taxonomy of learning. It helps to identify the level of learning that has taken place in terms of application to the workplace and assists the manager in recognising the level of learning in the staff member.

Figure 19 below shows the pyramid of learning (Anderson & Krathwohl):

At a basic level, learners are expected to remember what they have learned; understanding takes place at the second stage and by stage three they will be applying their learning to their workplace. For many staff members this will be the furthest level they will achieve; however, some learners will then progress through the other stages towards becoming expert in that particular area.

The effectiveness of training is easier to measure than the effectiveness of coaching. Training typically involves learning a skill, knowledge or competency and is therefore a measurable quantity. Coaching, however, usually involves behavioural terms and attitude. Although improvements or changes in behaviour may be observed, it is harder to assess.

Feedback is essential in evaluating development effectiveness, identifying and considering the improvement and change between what was happening in the previous situation and what is happening in the current situation. The CAR model will help in measuring effectiveness of both training and coaching:

> **C** – current situation: what is the learner's current level of skill or knowledge prior to completing the development. This will include analysis of the learning gap and the personal development objective identified.
>
> **A** – activity that has taken place needs to be reviewed. Learners should reflect on their learning and consider ways to transfer this to the workplace in their own role.
>
> **R** – reviewing both activity and workplace application. Managers should provide feedback and together with staff member evaluate the effectiveness of the development and look at ways of reinforcing it.

Personal Development Plan

This is the plan that documents the proposed learning, the activity and how it will be measured. Most companies will have their own format; however the one on the next page will provide a basic structure:

Personal Development Plan

Staff name:	Position:
Manager's name:	Date:

Learning Need

Learning Activity

Learning Objective (SMART)

How will you know learning has been effective?

Do you need any support? If so, who will this come from?

Giving Feedback

Giving feedback has been touted as one of the most important skills that a manager needs. It requires considerable skill to be able to give effective and meaningful feedback and is often under-estimated as a management skill.

Feedback is given to help people to develop an awareness of what they are doing, how they are doing it and the effect it has. Good managers will give plenty of encouragement and praise to provide reassurance. However, it is important to balance positive reinforcement with constructive feedback to enable staff to develop. Too much positive feedback leaves feelings of insincerity unless peppered with constructive ideas for development.

Feedback is not given to make you feel better – it is given to facilitate development and is an important component of learning which is easily lost when there is no review or feedback.

Timing is crucial and it is best to give feedback as soon as possible, having given the manager a few moments to prepare what they are going to say and how they are going to say it.

Rudyard Kipling referred to his 'six honest serving men' in many different situations: These are what, where, when, how, why and who. Consider Kipling's Men in giving feedback:

- **What** is the feedback you are giving? What is your message going to be? What do you want the staff member to think / feel / do? What alternatives do you have to help them explore?

- **Where** are you going to give this feedback? All feedback is best given in private to avoid embarrassment and problems within a team.

- **When** are you going to give the feedback? It is best to give this as soon after an incident as possible, when you've had time to prepare. Consider the timing and the possible impact on the individual – giving feedback at the end of the day may cause the person to worry during the evening.

- **How** are you going to give them the feedback? Consider the words you are going to use and be clear and concise. Too many managers give feedback wrapped up in waffle and extraneous words which leave the staff member confused as to what the message is.

- **Why** are you giving feedback? You should only be giving feedback if you feel you can help someone to develop and they will welcome the feedback.

- **Who** are you giving feedback to? As a manager you are responsible for giving feedback to your staff and your team. You may feel comfortable giving feedback to other people, peers, your manager.

A few tips in giving feedback:

- Focus on the behaviour you observe and not the person

- Describe what happened in straightforward, non-judgemental language

- Give specific, relevant examples

- Share ideas and give information but encourage the individual to come up with suggestions for moving forward

- Explore alternatives honestly, but let the individual make decisions on direction

- Look for commitment to specific changes in behaviour

- Where required, provide evidence

- Consider how much feedback to give – remember the bad news sandwich: one piece of positive feedback, one piece of constructive and one piece of positive

- Avoid using negative words like 'wrong', 'inappropriate', 'bad', 'incorrect' and 'failure'

- Always finish on a 'high' so the individual doesn't leave feeling let down

- Focus on the positive and encourage the learner to see any mistakes as learning experiences. "Experience is the name men give to their mistakes" (Oscar Wilde)

Coaching

Another tool used in developing people and increasingly being used in managing staff is coaching. It is important to differentiate coaching from other development mechanisms and to understand when and how it may help individuals.

Firstly, let's look at what coaching actually means and how it differs from other skills managers will use.

Coaching is improving performance through a range of learning experiences to identify areas for improvement. This may involve helping someone to solve a problem, learn a new skill, address a difficult area or achieve a goal. Just as a coach will act as a vehicle to move people from one place to another, coaching is a technique to enable individuals to move forwards in their career. There are a variety of different types of coaching which include business coaching, performance coaching, sports coaching and life coaching.

Other skills used by managers which are similar but not the same as coaching include:

- **Advising** – giving opinions or information which may or may not be taken. Guiding or giving advice based on your own experience.

- **Instructing** – teaching others or giving instruction on how something should be done. This includes demonstrating practical skills.

- **Counselling** – encouraging others to take responsibility for a problem. It focuses on past experience.

- **Mentoring** – less formal, combines elements of all the above. Aimed at helping people to realise their potential.

Coaching is based on the premise that the answer lies within the individual and it is through careful questioning provoking thought and reflection that the individual will come up with potential solutions. One of the benefits of coaching is that the individual is going to be more committed to something which they came up with rather than something they are told to do.

The coach does not need to be an expert in a particular area – coaching is a skill which can be developed and is a useful part of a manager's toolkit as it helps to empower individuals and over time give them the skills to think through situations and come up with answers for themselves.

There are many coaching models available which provide a structure on which to base a conversation or a coaching experience.

The SOAR technique has been developed to provide a model on which managers can base meaningful conversations with their staff, seen below in figure 20:

Situation

Outcome

Action

SOAR

Success

Review

Based around four stages, the manager moves through the stages questioning the individual at each step and moving on to the next stage as the staff member is ready

S – situation. Assess the current situation for the individual. This includes exploring any problems or concerns they have, together with any vulnerabilities they may feel in terms of their situation or their confidence. Other areas to cover are skills, knowledge, experience, gaps and attitude. You may also want to consider if they have any skills they use away from the workplace that are transferable.

O – outcome. Identify the goal, objective or outcome. This may be a long-term outcome which requires refinement and setting of interim short-term goals or a specific short-term goal. The individual should own this process and set the goal. The outcome should be SMART. The outcome should also be explored in terms of impact in other areas (ie promotion may have an impact on personal / social life as well as business). Goals should be Well Formed Outcomes (WFOs) and include ways of how the individual can measure their success or degree of achievement.

A – action. Consider the various options available to achieve the defined objective. Each option should be carefully evaluated in terms of the individual's ability to achieve, resources required, obstacles and support. Once each option has been considered, the individual should select the 'best fit' option and explore any support required to undertaken the action. The difference between a dream and a goal is a plan – this is the stage during which the individual should be defining their strategy towards achieving their goal.

R – review. Look at results, check how the individual is doing and review how things are going in terms of achievement, any obstacles and strategies f, consider what has gone well, what has not gone well and what has been learned. Examine the learning process and how this can be applied in other areas. Consider the amount of support that has been required or may still be required.

Learning Bite:
For each stage of SOAR, think about the questions you might ask an individual.

Conflict Management

What is Conflict?

The Cambridge dictionary[xxxiv] defines conflict as "*an active disagreement between people with opposing opinions or principles*". Equally it can be defined as a disagreement between parties who perceive a threat to their interests or needs resulting in a difference in the positions of those involved in the conflict. It is frequently disagreement resulting from misinterpretation or misunderstanding which then clouds and confuses the true issue with each party wanting their own way.

Conflict may involve just two people or a number of staff. However, if it is not swiftly resolved it becomes an issue which affects the team or department at work and at a social level so other team members feel obliged to participate in the conflict and assume 'sides' which exacerbates the conflict.

Conflict is part of organisational life and when viewed positively can be seen as an opportunity to develop the team, widen their knowledge and awareness and promote good team working relationships. However, it is frequently perceived as negative.

Managers should be able to foresee some of the potential areas of conflict which occur within the work environment itself, use these to grow the team and resolve problems before they escalate. For example, managers should be able to identify periods of increased workload that may cause stress, areas of the working environment that may create conflict or a lack of policies and processes for dealing with situations leaving staff unclear.

Other causes of conflict in the workplace may include:

- Different goals

- Sources of power (or perceived sources of power)

- Jumping to conclusions

- Different values

- Personality clashes

- Competition between the two parties

- Jealousy

- Inability to do job and lack of confidence

- Poor management or incorrect management style

- Different perception of the problem, situation or issue

- Poor communication

- One party trying to take advantage of the other

- Contrary attitudes

- Different opinions

- Low credibility and respect

- Hostility

In addition, interpersonal friction can be caused at work by:

- Perceived differences – race, religion, political systems, departments at work

- Inability to communicate – language barriers

- Biological orientation

- Spatial relationships – need for personal space and overcrowding causes conflict

- Bullying – this can either be bullying from management or from peers

- Harassment – sexual and other forms of harassment will cause conflict at work

Whatever the cause, the manager needs to be alert to problems and identify ways to solve problems before they escalate.

Stages of Conflict

There are four stages of conflict. Something that starts out as very minor quickly grows and becomes out of control. For this reason, the quicker a problem can be resolved, the less impact the conflict will have. If a problem reaches the highest stage - violence - it can lead to employees striking, picket lines, physical abuse and it becomes much harder to resolve.

- **Stage One - Irritation** – minor little niggles that irritate which you could do without. However, they can be difficult to ignore and tend to accumulate. People are beginning to feel dissatisfied and motivation decreases.

- **Stage Two - Annoyance** – increased problems, causing some difficulty and stress. Initially objections are voiced logically and rationally. Atmosphere becomes tense at work.

- **Stage Three - Anger** – emotions begin to take over. People feel hurt and treated unfairly feeling victimised. Verbal abuse will become stronger and people will begin to take sides.

- **Stage Four - Violence** – the conflict is out of control. Both parties now want to win by any means. Irrational thought takes the place of logic and common sense. Verbal abuse increases and there may be examples of physical violence as people lose control.

Although conflict can have both benefits and disadvantages in a work situation, it needs to be handled as soon as possible to prevent escalation. When handled badly, the cost is high – to the individuals, the team and the organisation because:

- It diverts attention away from the real issues
- People become too emotional and say things they do not mean and which are inappropriate to the issue
- One or both parties become so frustrated that it is much harder to resolve the situation

Conflict is generally dealt with through negotiation. There are three possible outcomes in a conflict situation. These are:

- **Win / Win** – both parties realise that they each have to give something in order to reach a satisfactory conclusion. Both parties leave with the feeling that they have been successful to some degree.

- **Win / Lose** – one party wins whilst the other loses. This leaves behind bad feeling, resentment and the relationship will have lost a degree of trust

- **Lose / Lose** – no agreement can be reached and both parties leave without a satisfactory conclusion. Both have therefore failed.

The only alternative to the above is where both sides pretend there is no issue and continue as best they can, but this is prone to further problems and unlikely to succeed in the longer term.

Handling Conflict

Logical reaction is often difficult but can help diffuse difficult situations. It can help to:

- Step back to view the situation more clearly

- Try to remove emotion and respond calmly

- Look at ways to move the situation forward

- See things from the other person's viewpoint

- Realise it is not possible for everyone to agree on everything

Styles of Conflict Handling

Each individual will have different strategies for dealing with conflict which may depend upon their personality, the situation or other factors. Most will have a preferred style which will help them to meet their needs. Recognising your own and others' preferred styles helps to resolve situations rather than cause further irritation and frustration.

These are the five main styles which people tend to adopt when faced with conflict:

The Shark – known as the 'forcing' or 'competing' style. Sharks will try to use their power to force others into submission and accept their solution. They are driven by their goals and fear failure. Relationships are less important to them, winning is all and they work on the assumption that conflicts are resolved when there is a winner and a loser. Sharks want to win – they crave the respect this will give them and the sense of achievement they will feel. They attempt to resolve conflict by attacking the other party, forcing them into intimidation. It is unco-operative, aggressive and most frequently results in a win/lose situation where the shark wins. The exception to this is when two sharks come up against each other and in this case one shark will frequently turn turtle preferring to retreat than engage in a battle they risk losing.

The Turtle – this is known as the 'avoiding' style in conflict. Turtles do not want to engage in argument or disagreement of any kind. They withdraw into their shells, prepared to give up their personal goals and relationships. Wherever possible they will avoid situations where there is likely to be conflict and people who engage in conflict or are argumentative. Turtles feel helpless and believe it is easier to withdraw emotionally and physically than face conflict. It is unco-operative, passive and usually results in a lose-lose conclusion.

The Teddy Bear – this is known as the 'accommodating' style. Teddy bears seek harmony, they like to be accepted, valued and liked by everybody. Their relationships are more important to them than their goals and they will sacrifice their own goals for other people to be happy and to preserve the relationship. They believe conflict should be avoided as it can damage relationships. This style is co-operative, but unassertive and will usually result in a win / lose conclusion with the teddy losing.

The Fox – this is known as the 'compromising' style. Foxes seek a compromise, they don't see the point in long drawn-out collaboration and want to move on. They are equally concerned with their goals and relationships but are willing to give up part of their goals and encourage the other person to do the same. They look for middle-ground solutions where both sides will gain something and should be satisfied with the outcome. Although it is often the only viable way to reach a solution, it only partially satisfies each party's needs. It is semi-cooperative and semi-assertive and will usually result in a win / win situation if both parties leave happy with what they have achieved. However, if both parties leave unhappy, the situation becomes lose / lose.

The Owl - this is the 'collaborating' style which is usually seen as the most appropriate style of resolving conflict. Owls value their own goals and relationships. They see conflict as a problem to be solved and they will seek out solutions to achieve both their own goals and the goals of the other person, whilst retaining the relationship. They will use a structured approach to resolve conflict by identifying the problem, finding out the other person's views, stating their own and seeking the best way for both to move forward so that relationships are preserved. They try to begin a discussion that identifies the conflict as a problem. It is both co-operative and assertive and will most usually result in a win / win conclusion

---

Learning Bite:
Consider the four styles and identify which is your preferred style. When does this work well for you? When do you need to use a different style and why?

Management Responses to Resolving Conflict

Every manager has their own conflict handling style depending on their personal management style. For example, a directive manager may be forceful or competitive in resolving conflict whereas a consulting manager may be more collaborating or compromising in their method of handling conflict.

Typical management responses may include one or more of the following:

- **Dismissal** – getting rid of the employee is a drastic way of resolving conflict and should really only be used as a last resort.

- **Disciplinary procedures** – this would need to fall in line with company policy and current legislation, but can be effective as a last resort.

- **Denial** – this is an avoiding tactic which is unlikely to work because it is ignoring the problem and hoping it will go away on its own. A manager using this method is likely to lose the trust and respect of their staff.

- **Suppression** – trying to suppress the problem or the difficult people.

- **Dominance** – using the power and authority to win. "Might over right."

- **Compromise** – this would involve listening to both parties and finding a middle ground.

- **Collaboration** – this would also involve listening to both parties and trying to work with both to find a mutually satisfying solution.

- **Co-operation** – encouraging co-operation which would in turn help with team dynamics.

- **Discussion** – explore areas of conflict and look at ways to resolve.

- **Mediation** – bring in another person trained in mediation who can help both parties resolve their differences.

Conflict is less likely to occur in an open working environment where staff feel able to communicate with each other and with management. A positive working environment promotes individual development without jealousy or competition.

Creating harmony within a department or within an organisation is a key feature of both an organisation's structure and a manager's style.

What is Motivation?

"Motivation is defined as the process that initiates, guides and maintains goal-oriented behaviours. Motivation is what causes us to act, whether it is getting a glass of water to reduce thirst or reading a book to gain knowledge. It involves the biological, emotional, social and cognitive forces that activate behaviour"[xxxv]

Motivation can be defined as the inner desire to achieve certain goals or objectives. Therefore to motivate someone is to provide the stimulus to encourage them to achieve.

Remember the saying "you can lead a horse to water, but you cannot make it drink". In the same way, you can give staff tasks to do, but you need to stimulate their interest for them to achieve successfully.

Most people want to do a good job and to do it well; the manager's challenge is to help them to do it. Employees will only commit to goals and objectives if they see the value in them and really want to make them happen. This cannot be done through simply issuing orders, supervising or delegating – it needs to be done through motivating.

Too frequently we make the mistake that to motivate someone is something we actually do to them. In reality, motivation is about finding out what makes people tick and using this knowledge to encourage them and tune in to their self-motivation. Managers and organisations cannot be all things to all people and there will always be people who lack the motivation they need in their role possibly due to the nature of the role, the fit to their personality and the culture within the team or organisation. This is important for managers to recognise so they do not feel they have failed staff in some way.

People are motivated in different ways and by different techniques. Some people are motivated by **goals or objectives** and see these as a challenge – the harder the goal, the greater the challenge and the better the performance. This is often called 'managing by objectives' (MBO).

Others are motivated by **rewards** – this can mean different things to different people but falls into two different categories:

- **Intrinsic** – these are the positive feelings that make people feel good inside and include contentment, pleasure, feeling wanted, satisfied, loved and proud of achievements.

- **Extrinsic** – these are tangible rewards and may include time off, bonuses, salary rises, promotions, recognition, rewards, company cars and incentives. Extrinsic motivators may include the 'carrot' or the 'stick'. Whilst the carrot is viewed as a reward, the stick is viewed as a punishment or threat. In some organisations, staff will be motivated by the fear of failure and losing their job.

Motivating staff can be a challenging aspect of the role and when times are difficult, staff are more likely to be demotivated. Managers need to recognise the classics signs of demotivation and address these as quickly as possible.

During times of uncertainty, reorganisation and change, staff are likely to feel vulnerable and demotivated. They fear that change is a threat either directly or indirectly to them and their role. Whilst uncertainty in some areas may be seen as a challenge and a motivator for some, for others it will be a demotivator. Signs of poor motivation include sickness, increased levels of stress, absenteeism, poor quality work and complacency in staff. There may be friction and conflict in a team which had previously worked well together as tempers become frayed and staff become demotivated.

Tackling these concerns quickly is essential and one way of doing this is to involve people, bring them together to make them feel valued and foster a sense of belonging. Involving people in change will make them feel important and will focus their energies on the change rather than on the worry of change. Problem solving or brainstorming as a team will help re-motivate and re-energise people. Keep the momentum going by empowering staff to own their ideas and take them forward.

Before you can motivate staff, you need to consider your own motivation and the messages you are giving to your staff. The following questionnaire will help you to identify how well you motivate your staff as a role model

Your Motivational Style

For each statement, tick if you do this on a daily basis:

Statement	Tick
I act as a role model for how I prefer my staff to behave	
I am willing to admit mistakes and take responsibility	
I do not punish staff who make mistakes, I prefer to use it as a learning opportunity for them	
I keep confidential information to myself	
I encourage my staff to come to me if they have a problem	
I trust my staff to complete their work to a high standard	
I delegate readily when it is appropriate to do so	
I treat all my staff fairly and consistently	
I believe that the way I behave towards my staff will influence how they behave towards each other	
I encourage staff to participate in development and training	
I participate in continual professional development to keep my knowledge and skills up to date	
I involve my staff in important decisions that affect the team when it is appropriate	

I am not afraid to tackle problems within the team or to discipline staff when appropriate	
I arrive on time for work and do not leave early	
I adapt my management style to each individual member of my team	
I set work objectives and personal development objectives with each individual	
I regularly appraise staff both formally and informally	
I provide regular and timely feedback to my staff	
I balance feedback between positive and constructive	
I show my staff I value them	
Total	

Now count your ticks. If you have more than 15 you are a positive role model to your staff and conscious of the impact you have on their levels of motivation. If you score between 10 and 14, you have the basics in place and need to identify areas to work on. A score of less than 10 indicates you have work to do in both managing and motivating your staff.

Learning Bite: *Using the results of your self-assessment questionnaire, identify two areas which you believe are a priority to work on. How are you going to do this?*

"What gets asked for gets done.
What gets measured gets done better.
What gets rewarded gets done best of all."

Step One – What gets asked for gets done

Employees with low self-esteem and poor motivation need fuller instructions when being asked to do something. They need to know what is expected of them, why it needs to be done, when by, what resources are available and what will happen if the work is not done. Always remember to say 'please' and 'thank you' and always give feedback and encouragement when people have done a job well.

Step Two – What gets measured gets done better

Setting objectives helps to focus the employee. Many people are motivated by goals or objectives as it helps them to focus and they feel a sense of achievement when the goal is achieved. Goals need to be set carefully so that they are both realistic and a little stretching to ensure staff feel sufficiently challenged.

Step Three – What gets rewarded gets done best of all

Employees need to be rewarded for good performance or for doing things outside their remit. This in turn encourages similar behaviour and performance in the future. Rewards needn't be large, just a few words of thanks is often sufficient, although more tangible rewards are appreciated. This acts as a motivator for the employee and also for other staff within the group.

In times of cut-backs it may be difficult to offer financial rewards or incentives, so finding alternative ways to motivate and reward is important. Consider low-cost options like 'employee of the month' or 'cake Friday' or special ways to recognise people and make them feel valued.

Several groups of training delegates were asked to write two things that motivated them on yellow post-it notes and two things that demotivated them on green post-it notes. These were then grouped on a flipchart and revealed that whilst a very small percentage of people are motivated by salary and money, most people are motivated by the work itself, by the people and by the provision of feedback and praise. Equally the demotivating factors showed that where the challenge of work is non-existent, there is conflict in teams and where there is little or no feedback from the manager, staff become demotivated and less productive.

Whilst recognition is important, managers should not reward all staff equally if they do not all work as hard – recognition and reward should be based upon performance. If there are incentives to aim for, staff need to be familiar with what they have to do to qualify for a reward or incentive and good communication is essential. Consistency is also important so that employees know where they are and what they need to do.

Learning Bite:
Consider ways in which you can motivate yourself and your staff.

There are many motivational theories used in management, the most popular ones are probably Maslow's Hierarchy of Needs, Herzberg's research and David McLelland's model all of which will help a manager to better understand their staff's motivational needs.

Maslow's Hierarchy of Needs

Abraham Maslow was a psychologist in the USA and he originally developed his famous pyramid, known as the Hierarchy of Needs, during the mid-1940s after extensive research. It remains one of the most popular models for understanding motivation both in personal and work environments.

Although Maslow died during the 1970s, his hierarchy of needs has been adapted into seven and eight stages by subsequent psychologists elaborating his original model. It is only the original five stage model that can be attributed to Maslow.

Maslow worked on the premise that we have different requirements from basic to higher needs and these need to be satisfied in turn beginning with the lowest level which looks at the requirements for survival. Only as we satisfy lower needs can we begin to look at satisfying higher needs concerned with personal growth and influence. If something happens to threaten our basic needs, all higher order needs are forgotten. Whilst as individuals we may achieve a higher level, this may be threatened if something in our life goes awry. For example redundancy, bereavement and loss may send us back to the lower levels.

Maslow's Hierarchy of Needs is frequently shown as a pyramid as in Figure 21 below:

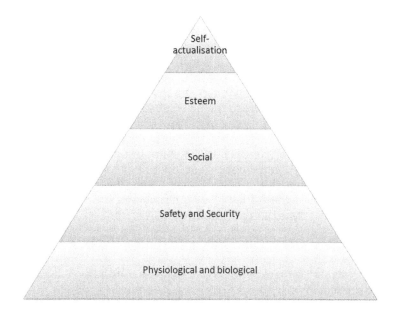

Physiological and biological needs – these are the most basic needs and form the foundation of the pyramid. They are psychological and include air, water, shelter, warmth, sleep, sex and food. All of these are seen as vital for the continuation of life and if these were removed our lives would be in danger. In some parts of the world fights take place to preserve these basic needs. Once our physiological and biological needs are satisfied we can move up to the second level:

Safety and security needs – these are required to help us feel safe from danger. Included are shelter, clothing, protection from the elements, order, law, stability, boundaries and personal safety and security. Once these are met, we move up to the third level:

Social needs – no man is an island and we all need to feel part of a family or a work group or a social group. We need friends, colleagues, mates and relationships. We need to feel loved and we need to feel that we belong. We want people to talk to, to share our joys and sorrows, hopes and fears. Once these social needs are met, we move up to the fourth level:

Esteem needs – this is our own personal status. Within our team, group or family we need to have a role that will provide us with our own individuality and identity. It gives us the ability to be ourselves and have our own personality. It reinstates our independence, our managerial responsibility, our own achievements and status. Once we satisfy our esteem needs, we move on to the highest level:

Self-actualisation – this is our own personal growth and development, our personal sense of fulfilment knowing that we are using our talents and gifts, and are achieving. We are where we want to be, we are completely satisfied and know that we have done and are doing the best we can.

As a manager, you may help your staff to develop confidence and motivation in the workplace through considering the application of the different levels to the working environment. For example,

- Level one (physiological and biological) may be satisfied through induction training and an introduction to the working environment and the facilities available.

- Level two (safety and security) may be achieved through the provision of a safe working environment, ensuring staff are paid on time, they have somewhere safe to store belongings and they feel secure in their workplace.

- Level three (social) will be helped by team working practices, regular meetings, involvement with colleagues and social activities.

- Level four (esteem) may be helped when managers provide regular feedback, guidance, development opportunities and appraisal.

- Whilst all of these will lead towards level five, this is the individual themselves. Managers can go so far towards motivating staff in the application of Maslow's hierarchy of needs; however, it is up to each employee to complete it.

Learning Bite:
Consider how you as a manager may use Maslow's Hierarchy of Needs to motivate staff in your team using specific examples for your department.

Frederick Herzberg

Frederick Herzberg's original research centred on 200 Pittsburgh engineers and accountants and has become one of the most replicated studies in the field of workplace psychology. His theory became known as the dual-factor theory or the hygiene motivation theory. He was the first to recognise that satisfaction and dissatisfaction at work nearly always arose from different factors, and were not simply opposing reactions to the same factors, as had always previously been believed.

He showed that certain factors truly motivate: these he called 'motivators'. Other factors lead to dissatisfaction and he called these the 'hygiene factors'. According to Herzberg, man has two sets of needs: one as an animal to avoid pain and two as a human being to grow psychologically.

His two-factor theory differentiates between:

Motivators – these provide positive satisfaction and include recognition, challenge, job satisfaction, personal growth, development and responsibility. They result from the intrinsic conditions of the job itself.

Hygiene factors – these do not provide positive satisfaction and may cause dissatisfaction if they are not present in the working environment. These include job security, salary, working conditions, staff benefits, company policies, management styles and items extrinsic to the job itself.

So Herzberg concluded that hygiene factors are required to avoid dissatisfaction in a role and motivators are needed to provide the stimulus to improve performance.

Herzberg's further studies[xxxvi] concluded that the top motivators and hygiene factors (in order of preference) were:

Motivators	Hygiene factors
Achievement	Company policy
Recognition	Supervision
Work itself	Relationship with boss
Responsibility	Working conditions
Advancement and promotion	Salary
Personal growth and development	Relationship with peers

So how does this help the manager in motivating staff? Firstly, managers need to ensure that the hygiene factors are met as far as possible to avoid dissatisfaction and, secondly, that staff need to be challenged in their roles and provided with regular feedback and recognition of their achievements.

David McClelland

David McClelland (1917-98)[xxxvii], a psychologist, studied motivation and developed the achievement need theory. His findings have been adopted in many organisations and relate closely to Herzberg's theory. He identified three types of motivational lead in his 1961 book, The Achieving Society:

- achievement motivation (n-ach)
- authority/power motivation (n-pow)
- affiliation motivation (n-affil)

These needs are found to varying degrees in all staff and managers, and a combination of these will characterise an individual's style and behaviour, both in terms of self-motivation and in terms of management and motivation of other people.

The need for achievement (n-ach)

The n-ach person is 'achievement motivated' and therefore seeks achievement, wanting to attain challenging, but realistic, goals to advance within the role. These people need feedback to help them to progress and recognition of their achievement. As individuals they require a sense of accomplishment in their roles.

The need for authority and power (n-pow)

The n-pow person is 'authority motivated'. These people want to influence others, to have power and to use this lead. They need to feel effective, want to make an impact and crave both personal status and prestige.

need for affiliation (n-affil)

e n-affil person is 'affiliation motivated' and is sustained by positive relationships. They are motivated by their interaction with other people, they want to be liked, well regarded and hold their place within teams. They work well in teams as they care about other people and promote friendly relationships.

Learning Bite:
Thinking about your team, how would you best define the motivation style of your staff based on McClelland's theory?

McClelland acknowledged that most people possess a combination of these characteristics, although some will have a stronger bias towards one particular motivation need which will have an impact on their behaviour and working style. For those in a management position, their personal preferences will influence their style of management. McClelland suggested that those with a strong n-affil motivation may be undermined as managers as their overriding desire is to be liked and to be popular which may influence decision making abilities in management. Those with a strong n-pow motivation will encourage a strong work ethic and a commitment to the organisation; however, their lack of people skills may detract from their ability to manage staff despite their attraction to leadership roles. McClelland concluded that n-ach motivation is probably the best driver for leaders although there can be an inclination to demand too much from staff without fully recognising that people are motivated by different drivers.

Douglas McGregor's XY theory, which we examined in some detail earlier in this book, is another important influence in motivational theory and considers the value of the most appropriate management style for individuals which will either help to motivate or demotivate staff.

There are a variety of other motivational theories all of which will have some benefit to managers; however, these three will provide an insight into how staff are motivated and how you, as a manager, can best motivate your staff.

Communicating

The dictionary[xxxviii] defines communication as "the imparting or exchanging of information by speaking, writing, or using some other medium". So communication is about giving information. However, it can really be defined as the relationship between the communicator and the receiver as this is essential in open and honest communication. Messages can be transmitted in a number of ways: verbal, non-verbal, electronic, written and pictures. One of the most powerful ways of communicating is through our body language and our eye contact.

Communication is the source of most workplace problems and misunderstandings. It can never be perfected and needs a lot more care and attention than we usually give. It has been defined as the greatest influence on the effectiveness and productivity of an organisation and is therefore one of the most important skills for managers to learn.

The organisational culture and structure will have an impact on the effectiveness and reliability of communication. Smaller companies tend to have flatter structures and communication tends to be easier. The larger the organisation, the more hierarchical and complex its structure, the more problems arise from communication. It is like playing Chinese whispers in the work environment – messages get misunderstood, wrongly interpreted and this will cause problems. The more levels of management in a company, the greater the chance for misinterpretation.

"Communication is the fabric which holds organisations together and the thread which comes apart" - effective communication is a vital part of modern organisations. All organisations depend on good communication in every aspect of their work. Most managers are good talkers. They possess strong verbal skills to negotiate, persuade and communicate what they want. The better they are at communicating, the more successful they tend to be. However, most people will over-estimate their ability as communicators and the accuracy of the message received. Although we think of communication in verbal terms, it is also about listening. Listening is not merely staying silent. It is the facility to monitor the environment, interpret other people's messages, scan people's reactions and promote communication.

Whatever media we choose, communication is a two-way process used to exchange information and ideas, pass on knowledge, share thoughts and feelings. It is an important part of any role and can have a serious impact on a business's reputation.

Evolving technology gives us greater scope for communicating – and therefore greater scope for misunderstanding. We need to consider carefully the most appropriate medium for communication depending on the message, the recipient, the importance and the timing.

An understanding of the dynamics of communication helps us to identify why it is so important and how easy it is to fail. Figure 22 below shows the communication process in a simplified version:

Stage One: Message content decided and put into code	Stage Two: Message is transmitted via chosen media (ie spoken, email, written)	Stage Three: Message is received and decoded by recipient

Stage one – we have a message that we want to transmit. This may be verbal, written or non-verbal. Subconsciously we put it into a code based on our understanding, our mood, how busy we are, how important the message is and who is receiving the message.

Stage two – we transmit the message in the chosen medium (ie verbal, written).

Stage three – the other person will received the message. They will then decode the message based on their understanding, their mood, their attitude towards the sender and the subject, how busy they are and how important the message is. The message received is therefore not necessarily the message that is sent – it is wide open to interpretation.

So we can consider that communication is about receiving messages encoded and requiring some translation.

"Most people are too optimistic about the accuracy of the communication process. Although writing and speaking are relatively easy, achieving understanding is much more difficult" (Boddy and Buchanan[xxxix]).

Communication Media

Today we have a vast array of media available to us for communication purposes. Sadly it has not improved the overall effectiveness of the message. Choosing the appropriate media is critical for the message itself – often we will choose the communication tool that suits us best. It may be sending an email, which is less confrontational and we prefer to avoid conflict.

Too often we feel that we need to have proof or backup of our actions to prevent later problems or attribution and therefore we prefer to send email or written communications.

All media have advantages and disadvantages and here is a snapshot of the key methods used in the workplace:

	Advantages	Disadvantages
Telephone (includes telephone conferencing)	• Personal touch • Voice, tone and non-verbal cues aid understanding • We can adapt our approach according to message and recipient • Ask questions, seek feedback and confirm	• We may speak – they may not listen • No visual body language • Some people talk too much • Some people interrupt and don't allow others to finish • Often imprecise leading to

	understanding	misunderstanding
Written (letters, memos and other documents)	<ul><li>Generates response as perceived as more formal</li><li>Provides a record of communication</li><li>Easily stored and accessed</li><li>Usually more precise</li><li>Generally more thought is given to written word</li></ul>	<ul><li>Sloppy writing, grammar or spelling gives wrong impression and may lead to misunderstanding</li><li>Over use of abbreviations, jargon, technical language</li><li>More formal may mean too impersonal</li><li>Subject to Data Protection Act</li><li>Needs to be accurate and relevant</li></ul>
Visual (meetings, one to ones, Skype, video conferences, presentations)	<ul><li>Draws and maintains attention</li><li>Usually simpler and more direct</li><li>Easy to read non-verbal cues (body language)</li><li>Greater reach than other media</li><li>Less ambiguous and opportunity to see reaction of</li></ul>	<ul><li>Cannot control others' perceptions and reactions</li><li>Sometimes the visual impact (particularly slides) may detract from spoken message</li><li>Can be seen as overused</li><li>Dependence on visual elements</li></ul>

	• other person • Opportunity for instant feedback	
Electronic (email, text, internet)	• Delivery is usually instantaneous • Ease of use – any time, any where • Quick to send and deliver communication • Provides a record of communication • Usually simpler • More concise than written • Reaches large audiences • Access when travelling	• Too impersonal • Overused leading to information overload • Lack of human contact means communication becomes detached • Sender has no control over ultimate destination of message • Lack of etiquette and use of text language causes offence

So all methods have both advantages and disadvantages. It is about choosing the most appropriate media for the message, the occasion, the recipient and your own preferences.

Most organisations will have guidelines around telephone answering, formats for written communication and timeframes for responding to communication from internal and external clients.

Email is becoming more frequently used. However, it is often abused leading to people taking offence and causing minor conflicts in the workplace that can easily be avoided. Consider introducing an email etiquette for your team (or your company).

Email Etiquette

The following provides a basic overview of email etiquette which can help to avoid misunderstandings:

- Be informal, not careless – check spelling, avoid text language

- Brief and concise without being blunt – one subject per email

- Avoid the option 'reply to all' and use cc and bcc considerately

- Never use all capital letters, use sentence case

- Use subject field for purpose

- Think before you use – are you avoiding personal contact?

- Open and close emails politely – always have a salutation and closing

- Avoid abbreviations like BW or KR

- Re-read any emails that are particularly important to ensure your message is clear and will not cause offence

- Don't send chain letters or junk email

- Use a signature that contains all appropriate information

- Clean up any unnecessary information before forwarding

- Take care with sending and forwarding – email is public and may end up anywhere

- Remain fair, consistent and unbiased in email

Presentations

Presentations are frequently used in business for giving information to a team, presenting proposals to higher management or clients and reviewing progress in projects. It is assumed that most managers will have the essential skills to deliver a presentation; however, for many, this is an area they find difficult feeling nervous and therefore not giving an effective presentation.

Whilst this is not intended to give you all the information required to deliver a professional presentation, it offers the basics to help in developing and delivering a presentation.

Successful presentations begin with thorough preparation. Begin by asking yourself the following questions – who, what, where, when, why and how – to gain the essential background information.

- **Who** – consider your audience, who are the people and how many are there? What do they know about your subject and how do they feel about it? Are they really interested in what you're going to be presenting? What is their WIFM (what's in it for me)?

- **What** – what is the purpose of your presentation? What are your key messages going to be? What information are you going to deliver and at what level? What do you want the audience to think, feel or do at the end of your presentation? What do you want to get out of the presentation? What additional information may you want to give in the form of handouts?

- **Where** – consider the venue for your presentation. What will the layout be and what equipment is available for you? What are your audio-visual requirements? How much space will you need? Will you need other equipment, for example, laptop, data projector, internet access? You will want to familiarise yourself with any equipment to avoid problems on the day.

- **When** – think about the timing of your presentation. Are you slotted onto a full agenda? If so, what is immediately before you? How long have you got for your presentation and how are you going to use this time most effectively?

- **Why** – why are YOU giving this presentation? Are you the best person to deliver this information? Are you giving a presentation to inform, to sell, to advise or to entertain? Are you trying to persuade someone on a particular topic? Do you need to sell a solution or product?

- **How** – how are you going to structure your presentation? What information are you going to give? How are you going to go about the presentation? How are you going to get your messages across? How will you know you have been successful?

Now you have the background information, you can begin to plan the presentation itself.

Every presentation should have a structure:

     10% - opening or introduction
     80% - body or main part of presentation
     10% - conclusion

Introduction – start by introducing yourself and make sure everyone knows who you are and why you are there before beginning your presentation. Think about your USP (unique selling point). People don't want to hear your life history, just a quick 30 seconds of who you are. This is your chance to establish credibility. Then introduce the topic and consider an opening 'hook' to make an impact that will get your audience's attention straight away. You could consider:

- A provocative or dramatic statement

- A controversial question

- Asking the audience to participate

- An audio-visual gimmick or cartoon (take care with humour)

- An attention grabbing quotation

- An object or prop of some sort which could include models, toys or something for the audience to focus their attention on

- A statement of need

Through your introduction you want to establish rapport with your audience and state your objectives.

The Body - this is the main part of your presentation. You need to decide how you are going to plan this to include your key messages. Keep the key messages to a maximum of three and link your key messages with bridges so that the presentation flows. Try to bring your presentation to life by using anecdotes, real life examples and asking questions to include the audience.

Modulate your voice and use a range of tones – don't forget the VAK learning styles covered earlier in this book and try to engage all your audience.

When preparing your presentation, remember to use familiar words (no jargon or abbreviations) and avoid overcomplicating your message. Always speak in the first person, keep sentences brief and use positive language. If you need to include any unusual language or foreign words, explain them carefully. Avoid putting too many numbers or figures on slides or in the presentation. Less is more when it comes to statistics and numbers. Avoid using too many PowerPoint slides – approximately one slide for every three minutes is a good guide and never include too many words on a slide. They are there for visual impact and not to provide the main source of information.

The Ending – finally close with a 'bang'. Recap and summarise your key messages, then conclude with a final statement that will grab your audience's attention. Lastly, thank the audience for listening to you and ask if there are any questions. Always allow time for questions at the end of your presentation and if you do not want to be interrupted during the presentation, say at the outset and ask the audience to keep all questions to the end.

You will want to have notes for your presentation, particularly if it is a subject you're not as familiar with. If you are nervous, notes can act as a comfort to you if you feel you may forget your words or key facts. However essential they are, they are only a supportive aid for you and should therefore only have your key facts so you are not tempted to read them.

You will develop your own preferred style of taking notes. Some people like to type or write their notes on paper copies of the slides, others like to have notes on A6 cards with one for each slide. If you do use cards, keep them together on a key ring so you do not lose the order. Some people like to use mind maps to prepare notes and have a visual structure for the presentation.

Nerves - if you're not nervous, there's something not right! Nerves add the adrenaline which brings your presentation to life. However, you need to be able to harness the nervous energy, use it to good effect and don't let the audience see you are nervous.

There are four types of ways that nerves affect us:

Blushing – this normally begins just as you are about to start and will make you feel uncomfortable, hot and embarrassed. Try to ignore your blushing, it will disappear as your begin to relax. Take a deep breath and try to relax.

Dry Mouth - your mouth will suddenly feel dry as you stand up to speak and you'll wonder how you'll manage to talk. Have a drink of water to hand and take a small sip before you begin – this will help calm your nerves and lubricate your mouth.

Shaking - if you're prone to shaking or trembling, avoid holding anything in your hands and never use a pointer. Memorise the first few sentences of your presentation so that you don't need to refer to your notes and you will begin to feel more comfortable. Place your notes on the desk in front of you to avoid shaking as you hold them.

Forgetting Words - this happens to everyone at some point! It helps to know your subject well, have concise notes and try not to lose your place. It may help to summarise to your audience so that you give yourself a chance to recap and remember where you were. If all else fails, admit it to your audience – you're only human!

If you can appear confident to the group, your nerves will go and you will begin to enjoy the presentation. The secret to nerves is rehearse, rehearse, rehearse so that you are as familiar and confident as possible.

You are presenting your subject and also yourself. Never forget that you are the most important visual aid for your presentation. You need to be credible and you will want to be respected. A guideline in dressing for presentations is to always dress one level up from your audience to help you gain respect and credibility in the room. Consider your body language – be open, honest and assertive. Stand tall and avoid walking around too much. In engaging your audience, ask questions and use the 'lighthouse' technique for eye contact by looking at each person for a second or so and then moving on so you are scanning the room and making everyone feel involved in your presentation.

After the presentation, reflect on how it went, what you did well and where you can improve for next time.

Learning Bite:
Consider presentations you deliver. How effective are you? How can you improve? When did you last get feedback on your presentation techniques?

Communication channels

We communicate with each other through three different channels:

- The words we say
- The tone we use
- The way we say the words (our body language)

Naturally, face-to-face conversation is much easier (or should be!) with less room for misunderstanding. We read each other's behavioural signals as well as listening to what we say and the way we speak. Telephone communication is therefore harder and requires more effort to transmit the same message.

Albert Mehrabian's studies[xl], which have often been misquoted, looked at the impact of verbal, vocal and visual cues on communication and found that words accounted for 7% of the message, vocal tone for 38% and visual (body language) for 55% of the message received.

Whilst his studies have been criticised for bias, these statistics go to show the greater value placed on our body language (including tone) compared to the importance of the words. In telephone communication, the vocal expression absorbs the body language accounting for 80% whilst 20% are the words alone.

Barriers to Communication

So let's look at ways to improve communication and maximise the message we want others to receive. Firstly, we need to look at the general barriers to effective communication. These include:

- **Environment** – inappropriate surroundings which distract the other person from fully focusing on the message. This could be down to noise level, too many people around, poor telephone connections, interruptions, physical environment. Consider how important your message is and ways of adapting your environment or the message appropriately.

- **Language** – may be a barrier in several ways including knowledge of the language, use of jargon, acronyms and abbreviations, accents and dialects. Consider the other person and their level of understanding to adapt the message accordingly, including using clear, concise language and vocabulary that is tailored to the recipient. Where people do not have English as their first language, speak slower (don't shout at them!) and look for their understanding.

- **Timing** – it may be an issue if the timing isn't appropriate for the message. Giving people bad news at the end of the day will cause them to worry during the evening. Just before lunchtime when people are hungry and energy levels are low is equally not good for delivering important messages. Consider the timing of the message and the other person.

- **Media** – choosing the most appropriate media for the message is vital. This will depend on the importance of the message, the recipient and you as the communicator.

- **Inconsistencies** – where there are inconsistencies in the message, particularly where it is passed down a hierarchical chain of command, the recipient will be confused and uncertain meaning the message is open to misinterpretation. Be consistent in the way you deliver messages particularly amongst your team so that everyone receives the same message.

- **Information overload** – giving too much information at once will cause the other person to feel overwhelmed with the volume and unable to focus clearly. They are less likely to fully understand the information. Consider ways to give information in bite-size chunks that people can easily digest and understand.

- **Personal style** – your own style as a manager may impact on the delivery of the message and the way it is received. This may be to do with the quality of your delivery in terms of voice, expression, tone and language. It may equally be due to your position or status in the organisation which may be seen as a barrier.

- **Personalities** – personality differences account for the key areas of conflict in the workplace. Communication is no exception and the rapport between the communicator and the recipient is important. It is one of the harder areas to overcome as we cannot change our personality to suit others. However, we can try to understand the impact we have and work to minimise any adverse effects.

- **Cultural differences** - may have an impact on understanding particularly in terms of body language, eye contact and appropriate behaviour.

- **Prior knowledge or expectation** – people may have a certain bias or a certain understanding of a topic and this will influence the message they hear and understand. Where there are certain expectations it can be very difficult to get your message across clearly.

- **Physical disabilities** – understanding someone's physical disabilities and finding ways to overcome these is essential. For example, if someone is deaf speak slowly and clearly, maintaining good eye contact as they may be able to lip read. For blind people, remember that speech is their main way of interpreting, so put appropriate expression into your voice. For people in wheelchairs and physically disabled, bend down to their level so that you can maintain eye contact and minimise the intimidation caused by physical height. Older people may not be deaf – don't make assumptions!

The effective communicator will identify barriers and have strategies in place to overcome these, seeking feedback to ensure messages are understood and information received.

Learning Bite:
Identify barriers you find in communicating with your staff or with others. What strategies can you use to overcome these and improve your communication?

Listening

Listening is a valuable business skill and is an important part of the communication process. It involves listening to the words, the way they are said and what is left unsaid. Being an effective listener is essential in management to keep the communication channels open.

Too often we listen at a superficial level – we hear the words, but not the message. We need to learn to listen with our ears, with our eyes and with our hearts and to consider, not just the message, but the meaning. Asking questions to clarify our understanding or to seek more information, providing feedback and summarising at the end of a conversation will help us to listen and ensure we hear.

Listening is an important part of customer service and the following guidelines will help you to become a more effective listener.

Some Simple Guidelines

- Use the other person's name (if you know it) - their title and surname is a sign of respect.

- Take time to listen to what they are saying – this means listening firstly to the facts (what they are saying) and then their feelings (how they are saying it).

- Use simple plain English, avoid jargon and offer clear explanations when asked.

- Treat everyone as an individual regardless of age, gender, religion, culture and health issues.

- Don't make assumptions about people or their needs.

- Always talk to the patient (not the carer or relative) and talk to them in the first person.

- Avoid using words which suggest pity for them.

- Avoid questions which are too personal.

- If someone looks as if they need help, offer and wait for them to accept – don't assume.

- Speak clearly and not too fast. Check they can understand and follow what you are saying.

- Look directly at the person and use facial gestures, body language and tone to emphasise what you are saying.

In summary, consider:

L   look interested

I   information seeking – ask questions

S   stick to the subject concerned and focus

T   test your understanding with feedback and summary

E   evaluate the message you're receiving to check interpretation

N   neutralise your thoughts against previous assumptions or expectations

Body Language

Body language is about understanding how people are feeling and what they are thinking from their gestures. Naturally behaviour patterns have existed for thousands of years, but it was only during the 20th century that it became an important area of study. It is incredible that while we have long been aware of the signals and body language of the animal world, that we, as humans, have been slow to accept the importance of body language in our daily communications with each other and in the workplace.

The concept of body language was given little attention until the 1960s when Desmond Morris[xli] increased awareness dramatically with his research into behaviour evolving from animals. We have an innate and subconscious ability to communicate through gestures and signals. For example, when we are happy we smile and our eyes shine; conversely when we are angry or sad our eyes are dull.

It is also human behaviour to mirror and match each other's posture and actions if we want to gain acceptance and as a way to acknowledge the other person. Mismatching occurs when the rapport between two people is non-existent or there is a degree of argument. Again, this is usually subconscious although we can learn to match others' gestures to build rapport.

There has been much debate as to whether body language is innate or learned. Certainly through studying people around us, we can increase our awareness, learn to read their signals and adapt our own behaviour accordingly. People in the public eye are taught to read and use effective body language although this then becomes a false premise for discussion and conversation.

To begin to understand body language, we need to understand a little about ourselves and how we react to other people. Firstly, consider the bubble around you – we have 'zones' which dictate our comfort levels with certain people. Our personal space changes according to the people are we with, our relationship with them and our mood. Generally there are three zones: closest to us is the 'intimate' zone and we only feel comfortable with partners, parents and children in this zone. Extending from around 45cm to 120cm is our personal zone – this is acceptable for friends and other people we know and feel comfortable with. It is often called the 'party' zone as socialising will often be in this area in tightly packed spaces. Finally our 'social' zone extends beyond this bubble and includes people we don't know well, don't like or don't feel comfortable with. When people invade the wrong zone, we feel intimidated and threatened, we do not respond positively to them and our 'flight' desire is stimulated.

These zones extend to the space around us and we become territorial about our spaces, our desks, chairs and equipment.

Cultural differences will impact on these zones and these behaviour patterns. People who have grown up in the city will often have narrower zones than those who have been brought up in the country.

In a similar way, we feel uncomfortable with tactile gestures unless we know the other person well. This can lead to misunderstandings and communication problems in the workplace.

Earlier in this book we looked at VAK language as a learning styles application. This applies equally to communication. If we have a visual preference, we prefer face-to-face communication, we like to see the other person and read their body language. Auditory people are happier communicating by telephone as they will read body language through vocal tone and emphasis. Kinaesthetic people are frequently misunderstood as they like to stand close to others and are typically tactile.

In the same way that we can match and mirror body language, we can identify the dominant sense of the other person and verbally match using predicates. A predicate associates words with dominant senses.

For example, a visual person may say "I see what you mean" and you can reply "That's clear to me too". An auditory person may say "I hear what you're saying" and a kinaesthetic person may say "I'm warming to that idea". Through careful listening we can identify people's preferences and tune in to develop rapport.

Learning Point
Refer back to the learning styles questionnaire you completed, consider the predicates you use and how this reflects your preference. Identify different phrases that you can use with others that feel comfortable to you.

An understanding of body language can help you to develop your communication style and there are many excellent books on the subject to guide you. As a general rule, the more open the body language the more honest the other person. Hands are a key indicator to how people are feeling and may be used as a 'barometer' for body language. People hiding hands are likely to be hiding something from you. Those who have folded arms, crossed knees and who hold folders or books against them are defensive.

Eye Contact

Eye contact is another important part of the communication process and one which will vary considerably between different cultures. Whilst in Western society it is considered polite and appropriate to establish eye contact, in other societies it is considered disrespectful to make eye contact, particularly between a man and a woman.

As a general rule, you should look at someone for between four and seven seconds before looking away. Any longer than this the other person will become uncomfortable and feel that they are being stared at. As you look away, take care to look to the side to break the contact without giving the message that you are not interested or fed up with listening. Eye accessing cues are barely noticeable but will appeal to the subconscious and can therefore give unspoken messages.

In the same way we have body zones, we also have eye zones which reflect the relationship between the two parties. In business, people will frequently look at the centre of the forehead and eyebrows – this is known as the business zone. The central part of the face including eyes and nose is called the social zone as this is where most eye contact will be. The lower zone including mouth and chin is the intimate zone and is one to be aware of! If someone looks at your mouth, it could be they are trying to lip-read; however, if their eye contact continues south, they are not listening to you – they have other things on their mind!

A knowledge of body language and eye contact is useful; it can be used to develop rapport and enhance communication. However, there are many other considerations to take into account when looking at developing communication skills. It is a skill that cannot be perfected, but can always be improved.

Understanding Change

Change is the only constant. It is never a single event. It is a continuous process that involves people and needs managing. Organisations are constantly changing and evolving to meet the fluctuating requirements of customers, clients and society. We live in a fast-moving environment and need to be continually prepared to change with these times, or risk being left behind. Whilst change should be exciting, many people fear change for different reasons and this makes implementing change a challenge for managers.

We will be looking at change management as a process in the next section; however, in managing people we need to be able to understand and manage change. Failure to manage change effectively means leaving people behind resulting in an unsuccessful change.

What is Change?

The Oxford dictionary[xlii] defines change as "an act or process through which something becomes different". So change is about making something different or altering something for a new purpose. However, change can be difficult particularly when it involves behavioural or attitudinal changes.

John F Kennedy claimed, "Change is the law of life. And those who look only to the past or present are certain to miss the future."

Change will be seen in many different areas and for each the level of impact will be different according to our role and the organisation in which we work. Some examples of change include:

- Seasonal change

- Process, policy, procedure changes

- Legislation

- Government initiatives

- Product or service offerings

- Organisation structure changes

- Organisation culture changes

- Role or job changes

- Mission or corporate objectives

- Personal change – marriage, divorce, bereavement, children

- Moving location (either home or office)

- Retirement

- Redundancy

- Technological advances

- Metamorphosis of nature

Change is driven by a variety of factors, some internal over which we will have some control as managers and others external over which we will have no control. Change drivers include:

- Growth

- Mergers and acquisitions

- Technology

- Competition

- Cost pressures

- Regulation

- Changing markets

- Economy

- Environment

- Climate

- Natural disaster

- War / conflict / strikes

Whilst many people are slow to embrace change, the benefits will usually outweigh the problems. Change is the way forward and will provide new opportunities to maintain or improve competitiveness. Change means organisations are better equipped to meet challenges and should generate a positive atmosphere. Organisations which change frequently possess a positive culture which proactively embraces and welcomes changes as the dynamic to prevent stagnation.

Understanding the depth of change and the potential effects is important to understanding the impact on people. Consider the depth of the change. Grade the change on a scale of 1 to 5 where 1 may be a minor change having little or no impact on a daily basis and 5 is a change which will have a major impact on staff.

Look at the following table to understand the impact of change at the different grades:

Grade	Impact	Example
1	Minor	Using a different supplier for printer paper
2	Superficial	Changes in the roles or processes of the team work
3	Shift	Restructure or reorganisation
4	Deep	Complete change of focus or mission statement for organisation, ie privatization of a public company
5	Major	Closure of organisation or merger with another company

The higher grade of change, the greater the impact on the team and the more effort and time required to implement the change.

Dealing with Change

Attitudes towards change will be influenced by previous experience. Surveys done through the years indicate the most frequent reasons for lethargy and negativity towards change are:

- Fear of the unknown

- Initiative fatigue - too much change resulting in too few benefits

- Change for change's sake

- Too busy to implement change

- Threatened by change either directly or indirectly

- Feeling exposed or out of comfort zone

- Influence by peers and colleagues

People deal with change in three ways depending on their personality, their previous experience, the depth of the change and their attitude towards the change.

- **Proactive** people will actively embrace change. They are positive towards change, will provide support and alliance and will influence peers to accept change.

- **Reactive** staff will accept the change when they have to. Whilst not as positive about the change, they appreciate change is required and will go along with it eventually. They will not be as supportive as proactive people but will generally not be a barrier to change.

- **Defiant** staff are actively against change. These are rebels who are negative towards change seeing it as a deterrent and will try to ignore the change. They are difficult to manage during change, requiring a lot of support and encouragement as individuals and may well have a negative impact on the rest of the team.

Understanding the process that staff go through will help you to understand, to empathise and to manage them through the process. This may be influenced by the way change comes about – whether it is a top-down process inflicted by higher management, or a bottom-up process influenced by the staff members themselves.

There are two cycles staff go through depending on their personality and their attitude towards the change:

The first is the more negative approach to change. Initially these staff will feel that the change comes as a shock and they will try to deny that it is happening or that it will have any impact on them as individuals or their role. In ignoring the change, they believe it will go away and as they begin to realise that the change is impacting they look for someone to blame. As other people begin to adapt to the change, they look to blame themselves wondering what they have done wrong to deserve this. At this stage, some may leave to seek new opportunities. Those who stay will begin to find ways to accept the change and their satisfaction will increase over time.

These people are harder to manage and will cause disruption and frustration in the team – they need more support, advice, guidance and help through the change both from the manager and the team.

The second approach is more positive. Initially these staff will welcome the change feeling that it is positive and will bring benefits. This first stage is called 'blissful ignorance' as they are optimistic without being fully aware of all the implications of the change. As realisation of the impact dawns, they will experience a stage of doubt and anguish: they now have all the facts and are feeling pessimistic towards the change. However, as they fully evaluate the benefits of change they will come to terms with the changes and become cautiously optimistic. This optimism will grow and these staff will become supportive and fully committed to implementing the change.

Understanding the two cycles is important for you as a manager. Understanding your staff is more important. Recognising that each individual is different and will react differently to change depending on previous experience and what is currently going on in their personal and professional lives, will help you to manage both your staff and the change successfully.

Aligning the change with the culture of the organisation and any sub-culture within the team is essential. Success depends on close alignment with the culture.

Any change programme must take account of three key factors. Firstly, the organisational culture and its readiness for change; secondly, the change programme itself; and thirdly the individual values and beliefs of the team. The greater the overlap between these three areas, the more successful the change programme. If there is no overlap the programme is likely to fail.

Communication is vital in managing change. There should be honest, open communication exploring potential impact with staff to help them understand and appreciate the benefits of change. We will examine ways of developing a communication plan as one of the change management tools in the next section.

Task Management

Task management is the third area of our management wheel and focuses on how you manage the task itself rather than the people. The four main components to this area include:

- **Business awareness** – your understanding of the organisation you are working in

- **Problem solving** – identifying symptoms, exploring root cause, developing and analysing solutions for implementation

- **Change management** – tools available to assist with managing change programmes

- **Business tools** – the different business tools available to you to help you plan, organise and manage projects and tasks

Some managers will have a definite preference for task management and will find this part of their role more enjoyable and satisfying.

Business Awareness

This involves understanding the organisation you work for, the industry sector you work in and an awareness of the external environment and economy and how this impacts on your organisation.

Organisations are enterprises that operate for a purpose and as a manager you need to understand the purpose, structure, culture, functional areas and managerial roles. All organisations will have an overall aim depending on the sector in which they operate. For example, companies operating in the private sector will have profit as a core purpose whilst those working in public sector should have breakeven as their main aim.

Types of Organisation

Organisations are businesses that are established with a particular goal or mission to accomplish. They can vary in size between one person and many thousands, all of whom work together towards a common aim.

> *"An organisation is a consciously co-ordinated social unit, composed of two or more people, that function on a relatively continuous basis to achieve a common goal or set of goals"* (Robbins, 1996)

Organisations can be either formal or informal.

> *"A formal organisation is the planned co-ordination of the activities of a number of people for the achievement of some common, explicit purpose or goal, through division of labour and function, and through hierarchy of authority and responsibility."* (Schein 1988)

Within larger organisations, a number of smaller organisations or teams exist. For example, the different trusts which sit within the NHS. Occasionally the goals and missions for these smaller organisations may clash or not fit with the parent organisation which can create problems.

Another example would be a large multi-national company with the parent company in the United States and a number of mini-organisations, each existing and functioning within their own right, in different countries around the world. The government, economy and law will impose different restrictions on the country organisations which may not fall in with the overall mission of the parent company. War and political pressures can also create large problems in these situations.

All organisations are collections of people. These people all have their own role to play towards the overall success of the organisation. The need for interaction and good communication is critical if the company is to grow and to be profitable.

There are many kinds of business, each with its own organisation structure to fit the company and its goals. These fall into four main categories:

- **Public Sector** – these are service companies which are owned by the state and are concerned primarily with the welfare and interests of the people, ahead of making money. They include central government departments, local authorities and councils, the civil service, the police and armed forces, public corporations (for example BBC) and nationalised services (for example the NHS). Since 1982 many previously public companies have been privatised including British Telecom, British Petroleum, British Rail and the utility companies.

- **Private Sector** – these are companies which are owned by individuals (one or more) and are concerned with making profit. The private sector absorbs many organisations including banks, insurance companies, law practices, manufacturing industries, oil industries, construction companies, retail and wholesale organisations.

- **Non-profit Making Organisations and Co-operatives** – these are companies or clubs which are established to meet a certain need. This category can be quite wide and includes professional bodies (examples are CBI and the British Medical Association), social clubs and trade unions. Co-operative societies were formed in the mid-nineteenth century to ease serious unemployment. The idea was for the society to purchase goods at wholesale costs and sell to members only at market price. The profits were then divided between members in proportion to the value of their purchase. Today these profits are distributed via trading stamp schemes.

- **Voluntary Sector** – these are organisations which have been established to meet a particular need. Most are charity groups whose aims are to raise money for a particular cause or groups of volunteers who provide a service to the public. This includes groups like Oxfam, the Samaritans and Childline.

Public Sector

Companies in the public sector were set up for the benefit of the public and are not operated for profit purposes, although they are run to break even financially.

Many companies were set up by Acts of Parliament for various reasons, including:

- Security – for example, police and armed forces

- Fundamental importance to the country's economy

- Social necessity – for example to provide education or health services

- Natural monopolies – for example, London Underground (although the number of these natural monopolies is declining due to privatisation)

Public corporations fall into four main categories:

Autonomous public corporations which are established to perform a particular function. Such corporations have limited parliamentary involvement, but fall under the control of a particular Cabinet Minister who is responsible for presenting an Annual Report and Annual Accounts to Parliament for discussion and investigation.

Nationalised industries are established to service the public and to meet the political and economic requirements which could not be achieved efficiently through private enterprise. The principal objective is to provide a public service without making a profit, but without incurring any losses. They are fundamental to the nation's needs and cannot be allowed to fail. Various organisations were nationalised for different reasons. For example, the NHS was established to provide a health service to everyone regardless of financial status. Other companies were nationalised to prevent an essential service falling into decline, such as British Rail before its privatisation. Others were nationalised to provide a more efficient service, such as Royal Mail.

Local government bodies are responsible for all community services including education, street cleaning, refuse collection, health services, drainage and maintenance of common ground. Each town or village falls under a borough which is governed by a local council. Their main areas of responsibility lie in community services, town planning, housing, police and emergency services.

Central government departments – these frequently change in both roles and responsibilities according to the current government. Each department or ministry is the responsibility of a Cabinet Minister who reports directly to Parliament. Ministries include transport, education, the Foreign Office, employment, environment, defence, health and the Home Office among others. Each ministry has an annual budget for expenditure which must be accounted for to Parliament in the annual reports and accounts by the responsible Cabinet Minister.

Private Sector

Usually a business starts as a small enterprise and grows into a larger concern, possibly becoming a multi-national conglomerate.

It is very unusual to find a large organisation mushroom overnight, but one example of this is Eurotunnel – a company formed with the specific objective of building the Channel Tunnel and in which the public were able to buy shares from the outset.

A business will normally begin in one of three ways:

- Sole trader (most common)
- Partnership
- Limited company (becoming more frequent)

Sole Trader – this is the most usual legal form for the smallest kind of business, involving one person who is the sole owner of the business. They work for and control their business, whether they are a market stall owner, a plumber or a freelance consultant. Often they will start out with a bank loan, but this does not mean that the bank has any share in the ownership of the company. The sole trader is personally liable for all debts and claims against their business. The profit is theirs and not shared with others, although they may have employees working for them.

Partnership – this can either be the second stage for a sole trader when he decides to take a partner into the business either for commercial or financial reasons, or it is more often the starting point for a small company. In these cases, two or more people invest their capital in a business and share responsibility. The minimum number in a partnership is two, but there is no quantified maximum number. The details of the partnership are set out in a partnership deed, although this is not a legal necessity. Profits and losses are distributed among the partners and they are all liable for all debts and claims against the business, both jointly and as individuals. Frequently, you will find 'sleeping partners' – these are people who have invested capital in the business, but who are not involved in running it and can therefore take no part in the active business. The majority of legal firms are 'partnerships' and there is no limit to the number of partners in a firm.

Limited Company – this is also known as a Limited Liability Company and is a business in which one or more individuals invest a certain sum of money and receive shares issued by the company. The individual's personal liability is limited to the nominal value of their shares. The assets belong to the business and not to the individuals. If one of the shareholders leaves, their shares are sold to someone else and the business continues. A limited company must be registered in accordance with the Companies Act.

Shareholders have voting rights, with the weight of their vote dependent on the number of shares (or percentage) they hold, so the more shares they hold, the stronger their voting right. Certain documents must be registered with the Registrar of

Companies and accounts must be lodged annually, together with a directors' report and an annual report.

A limited company must carry the abbreviation 'ltd' after its company name and incorporate its company registration number in any documentation.

Public Limited Company – this is the term used to define a private company which has grown to such an extent that the authorised share capital exceeds a specified amount (circa £50,000). The company is then 'floated' on the stock market which gives investors the opportunity to buy and sell shares publicly. The company is then owned by the shareholders and managed by directors. It is controlled by those investors who hold a majority of shares. When a private company goes public, it becomes registered as a public limited company and must use the abbreviation 'plc' after its name, in accordance with 1982 legislation.

All organisations are established with different purposes. The purpose or mission of most private sector organisations will be to make a profit. However, public sector organisations are structured with the purpose of providing a service to the public.

A **mission statement** sets out the overall purpose of the organisation. It describes what the organisation sets out to do in broad terms. It is a short written statement intended to guide the activities of the organisation.

The **corporate objectives** state in more specific terms, what an organisation is aiming to achieve. These are likely to change on an annual basis to take account of changing needs. They are established as part of an organisation's business planning cycle and set out the priorities to be achieved over the coming year or financial period. These may appear fairly broad and will then be broke down into specific, measured and timebound objectives.

The **values** of an organisation identify what is important to a company. These may be ethical or moral values by which the organisation identifies itself and its staff.

Organisational Structure

Structures vary from different organisations; however, all are made up of the activities required to achieve the organisational purpose. This will include supervision and management roles, resource allocation and the environment. Structures will be different depending on their objectives. However, the structure determines the way the organisation operates and, to a degree, the culture.

The organisational structure will affect the business of a company in two ways. Firstly, it acts as the foundation for standard operating procedures (SOPs). Secondly, it determines the level of staff involvement in decision making.

The most common forms of organisational structure include:

- **Hierarchical** – these tend to be bureaucratic and complex best suited to large organisations. A tall hierarchical structure will have many levels of management which may restrict the effectiveness of communication and the staff towards the bottom feeling valued. These are typical of public sector organisations and managers may have a relatively small span of control with only one or two employees reporting into them.

- **Flat** - this will have fewer levels of management and is very often seen in larger modern organisations where there will be only three or four levels of management, each with a greater number of staff reporting into each manager, which leads to better communication and increased motivation. These structures may be organised by division or by function.

- **Matrix** – this is a relatively modern structure which typically groups teams together into functions to work together under a project manager. The efficiency of a matrix structure depends on the effectiveness of the managers. Teams may be working together for short or long periods of time depending on the project needs and functions.

- **Virtual** – the newest type of organisation structure which is being recognised where staff work 'virtually' and rely on technology. This is like a network of people working for a central function or individual.

Organisations generally start out quite small and the structure grows as the size of the company grows. Within all organisations there will be direct reporting lines and dotted lines of responsibility. The larger and taller the organisational structure the more capacity for confusion and conflict in reporting.

Organisational Culture

A brief understanding of the organisational culture can help the manager in creating and developing a team.

Organisational culture is intangible and can be a difficult concept to grasp. It cannot be seen or measured, but is generally perceived and felt by employees as a thermometer of the organisation. Many people choose to work in a particular organisation because of the perceived culture that shows its values and beliefs.

Oakley and Greaves[xliii] describe the organisation culture as the 'glue' which sticks it altogether. They believe that if the organisation becomes fragmented for any reason, smaller sub-cultures develop and the 'glue' may no longer be effective.

Schein[xliv] used the iceberg model to illustrate the different levels of organisational culture and show that there are the visual aspects of an organisation but that much of the culture is invisible and beneath the surface. He stated that there were three levels:

The artefacts – this is the part of the iceberg above the water and visible to all. It may include the organisation's corporate objectives, customer set, environment, facilities and resources. It will also include policies and processes, written documents, disciplinary procedures and job descriptions. This will include the 'types' of staff employed, legends and myths within the organisation and traditions.

The values – this is the second layer which includes the ethical values of the organisation. Whilst some of these are visible and tangible, others are less overt. These include the mission statement, the code of ethics, the values and the beliefs that employees adopt and live by.

The basic assumptions – the third layer is the largest part of the iceberg and under the water, therefore covert. These factors are harder to measure but are the ones which have most influence over the way people feel and behave at work. They are the unconscious assumptions of the way things are done and will include communication patterns, staff attitudes and personalities, political and ethical behaviour, informal team processes and conflict.

In identifying the culture or climate of the organisation, we need to consider the contributing factors which will include:

- The organisational structure of reporting and relationships
- Hierarchy and reporting lines
- Roles, responsibilities and job descriptions
- Company policy
- Personnel practices
- Work flow and work loads
- Job design
- Management and supervisory styles
- Local customs and practices within departments
- Levels of trust
- Risk taking
- Social interaction
- Factions and politics
- Change management
- Communication
- Staff involvement and consultation

The culture comes from visible aspects of the company like its corporate objectives, mission and purpose, employment practices, customer service, policies and procedures. However, much of the culture is intangible and harder to define and this includes the way people behave towards each other, ethical practices, the unspoken 'rules' that people follow and team customs that develop.

Leadership styles are heavily influenced by corporate culture with some organisations showing a preference for task leadership and others for people leaders.

The culture of the organisation is determined by the way in which the employees within the organisation are encouraged to act and behave. The culture reflects the values and beliefs of the organisation and the people who work there and are frequently imposed from top down.

In a relaxed and open culture, information is available to all staff. Open door policy means that managers are seen as being available to staff at all times. In some organisations, managers are now encouraged to have a desk amongst their employees. Round tables are taking the place of formal desks to encourage an open, informal style. Informal relationships and first name terms encourage communication between all levels of staff. The atmosphere is comfortable and staff are generally more motivated and enjoy their work more.

In a closed and restrictive culture, the information is closely guarded and only available on a need-to-know basis. Managers have offices where the doors are frequently closed to discourage general chit-chat and informal communication. Meetings are generally scheduled and formal appointments required. People are more deferential to senior managers and less likely to express their views and feelings. Most communication is formal through written methods.

Relationships have a big impact on the organisational culture. In a working environment you will experience a range of formal and informal relationships.

Formal relationships are on a 'need to know' basis. They are formed with the people you need to be able to do your work fully. They may be internal (people who work for the same organisation as you) or external (people who work for other organisations). Formal relationships are usually quite cautious and restricted to a working relationship. They are based on mutual respect for each other.

Informal relationships develop over time and are most likely to occur within a team or close working groups. Informal relationships will extend into friendships and will demonstrate an interest in the people as people, rather than working colleagues, with an understanding of their home life, interests, values and beliefs. They will usually include a degree of social interaction.

There are considerable differences between the two cultures as can be seen in the following table, however most organisations will be somewhere in between the two.

Now the trend is towards an open culture, although elements of closed culture still exist in many organisations, typically those that are larger, more bureaucratic and publicly owned

Open culture	Closed culture
Relaxed attitude towards working practices and time keeping	Strict timekeeping in place with some staff required to check in and out
First name terms for all levels of management	Senior managers prefer to be addressed appropriately by surname
'Open door' policy providing access to managers at all times	Prior appointments need to be made for staff to meet with managers. Doors habitually closed to visitors
Open plan areas with fewer enclosed offices and where these exist, they tend to be glass-based walls	Managers have offices away from the staff promoting hierarchy
Round tables for managers in lieu of formal desks	Desks which stress the manager's hierarchical position
Open communication	Communication tends to be more formal
Flexible working patterns	

Where the corporate culture is not aligned with team cultures, sub-cultures develop which can cause conflict.

Charles Handy[xlv] linked organisational culture with organisational structure and defined four distinct types:

Power Culture (or Club Culture) - this is usually illustrated as a web and is frequently found in small to medium-sized organisations which are easily controlled by one person. The 'boss' is typically seen as the spider in the web controlling all the threads radiating from the centre and wanting involvement in everything. There are few rules, little bureaucracy and decision making is swift.

The power culture is managed by a leader who leads by reward. The power is centrally maintained and the organisation's effectiveness depends on trust and communication between staff.   Decisions are made quickly and usually centrally. Much is based on trust and affinity. Many companies with a power culture are young and entrepreneurial with few rules or procedures, very little bureaucracy and little documentation. The culture tends to be irrational, benevolent and impulsive although it may also be seen as cruel. Flat hierarchical structures are typical of power cultures

Role Culture – this is usually depicted as a Greek temple with a number of columns representing the pillars of strength in an organisation. The pillars are strong in their own right and may well be known for their efficiency. The organisation depends on the way in which work and responsibility are allocated, rather than on individual personalities. This culture depends on a hierarchical structure with several layers of management controlled from the top. It is managed through traditional roles with a CEO at the helm supported by a Board of Directors.

Policies and procedures govern working practice and people are defined by their roles. Bureaucracy is prevalent, decision making is slow and change is hard to implement. There are many rules and policies which form the backbone of the organisation. These organisations rely on reliability and stability, they find change and crisis very challenging and change will take a long while to embed. These companies are paternal and will 'look after' the staff to ensure they can work effectively. Tall hierarchical structures are typical of role cultures.

Task Culture – this is typically very job-oriented with the focus being on the task in hand. It has been called a 'net' as the strands vary in strength and thickness. Much of the power and influence originate at the knots of the net and does not come from the top. It is usually a flatter or matrix structure where teams tend to be equal and specialist. Everyone works together to ensure the task is performed. This is a typical problem-solving culture and power comes from expertise and specialisms rather than positional authority. Decisions are usually made together through consensus.

Staff are valued for their involvement and success is based on finding solutions to problems. Where employees possess expert knowledge or skills, they will have influence. This culture is frequently found in project management and facilitates easy working relationships with good communication. A company with a task culture aims to bring together the right people, the right skills and the right resources to get the job done. A matrix structure is an example of task culture.

Person Culture (or free culture) – this organisation focuses around an unusual concept where people work autonomously rather than co-operatively. There is very little structure and hierarchy. Decision making tends to be on an individual basis. It has been represented as a cluster of stars loosely gathered in a circle. Examples may include legal or professional partnerships. This is a very democratic culture, there is no real leader and management is seen as a chore. Promotions, selections and rewards are decided by peers. The person culture can be exhausting to deal with and is limited to the lifecycle of the people within the organisation and is therefore temporary.

However, culture is not as simple as that! Every organisation will have a number of cultures and sub-cultures with different management and leadership styles within each. The right culture is needed for the right job – the club culture would never work within a finance department.

As a manager you will want to encourage the appropriate environment and climate for your team to thrive and be effective. To do this, you will need to be a role model, exemplifying behaviour that you want to encourage in your staff and recognising positive behaviour in others. Maintaining open and honest communication helps to inspire a positive environment.

This provides a brief overview of the organisational culture which influences the team dynamics and leadership styles.

Learning Bite:
Consider the organisation you work for – do you believe it has an open or closed culture? Considering Handy's model, which do you believe is the prevalent culture?

Problem Solving

A problem only exists if there is a difference between what is actually happening and what should be happening. One of the biggest hindrances in problem solving is jumping to conclusions and assuming solutions will work without accurately defining the cause of the problem. This is similar to putting a sticky plaster over a cut without first washing it and seeing if there is any grit in the wound – it is a short-term solution that will not work. Too often we look at solutions without really defining the problem resulting in ineffective solutions for incorrectly defined causes.

There are eight steps to successful problem solving and these are:

Step one – awareness of the issue and understanding that there is a problem

Step two – identification of the symptoms

Step three – root cause analysis

Step four – consider potential solutions through brainstorming or creative thinking techniques

Step five – analysis of solutions and any potential implications

Step six – decision of solution, planning activities and timeframe

Step seven – implementation of solution

Step eight – review solution and consider if it has solved the problems

We will look at each of these steps in more detail, having already identified that there is a problem.

Identification of Symptoms

When a problem is highlighted, you need to start by asking questions to find out the required information to enable you to identify the symptoms and look at the root cause.

Consider the following six stages to defining the problem:

Stage	Action required
1	Identify the symptoms of the problem – ask questions to find out what is happening, who is it affecting, what is the impact, how is it happening and frequency. Find out all the facts.
2	Do your research and find out all the facts. Involve people with different perspectives who will offer a different view.
3	If you find the problem difficult, it may be that you are too close. Leave it alone for a few days and return to it with a fresh mind.
4	Look outside the problem to find out if anything else had changed which may have had an impact.
5	Do a root cause analysis to identify the true cause of the problem
6	Determine if the problem is minor and therefore not worth solving, or how much effort is required to resolve the problem.

Root Cause Analysis

Root cause analysis is essential in finding out the true root cause
of a problem and then looking at resolving it. It is a process
which requires you to continually question and ask 'why?' until
you find out the true cause of the problem, the root of a problem.
Identifying the root cause is vital in finding the right solution – so
that you can treat the root cause and not the symptoms.

Kipling's Men provides a framework of questioning to ascertain
the root cause. Asking what, where, when, why, how and who
and then continue with why, why, why until you identify the root
cause.

Another tool used to identify the root cause is Ishikawa – the
fishbone diagram. There is more information about Ishikawa in
the chapter on Business Tools later in this book.

Finding solutions

Albert Einstein claimed that "We can't solve problems by using
the same kind of thinking we used when we created them".
Often we are prevented from finding the best solutions to

problems by barriers we impose ourselves. These may include making assumptions, stereotyping people or situations or superficial analysis of the facts. We may have mindsets that hinder our thinking, or we may feel stupid engaging in creative thinking or lateral thinking, particularly if we have a logical mind.

As individuals, we usually have a preference for using one side of our brain. People who are more left-brain dominant are logical thinkers who like analysing and evaluating ideas. They are realistic and like to work through problems in a sequential, rational way. Whilst excellent at evaluating ideas, they are not always good at creating solutions. People who are more right-brain dominant are more imaginative and enjoy exploring different options. They are intuitive, good at producing lots of ideas and working randomly. Generally an idea that is generated by the left side and endorsed by the right side of the brain will prove to be a more effective solution!

There are many different tools used in problem solving, although the most popular one is probably brainstorming, which we will look at in some detail. Other tools include:

- **Nyaka** – which comes from the French N'y a qu'a (all you have to do), is a tool which is best used in a group setting and uses people's natural critical ability to identify the defects of a product or situation and for each find a solution. To use Nyaka with a team, you may begin by electing a scribe and setting a time limit. The scribe will then split the paper into two columns. The left hand column will be headed 'defects' and the right hand column 'solutions'. The team then begin by listing all the defects and then working through a solution for each one. Groups will usually reach consensus quite quickly and find a solution.

- **Trigger cards** – these are cards with different pictures (objects or animals) which are used as part of the problem solving process in a group or by individuals. The group or individual will select a card at random and use this as a trigger to discuss the problem. For example, if a card showing the Eiffel Tower is selected, the group will then identify connections between the problem and the Eiffel Tower. This will help look at the problem in a different way and work towards a solution

- **Mind mapping** – developed by Tony Buzan, Peter Russell and Mark Brown in the 1970s this is a very effective tool for problem solving and note-taking as it allows the mind to break away from linear lists and think randomly, generating different ideas. Derived from brainstorming, it can be used by a group or by an individual. You begin with a large sheet of paper and lots of coloured pens. The problem is put in the middle of the page (usually in a cloud or bubble). Main ideas are then put in bubbles around the outside and connected to the central problem with lines – these are the 'trunks'. Next from each main idea, you 'branch' out with sub ideas again connected by lines and then possibly into small ideas as 'twigs'. Whilst most people prefer words, pictures are very effective and colour certainly helps to bring the mind map alive. Once completed, associated ideas can be linked by dotted lines

- **Brainstorming** – probably one of the best known creative thinking techniques used in problem solving. The objective of brainstorming is to encourage people to come up with as many ideas as possible to find solutions to problems. It can create logical solutions, creative ideas and original ways of looking at a problem. Although any number of people between two and 20 can participate in a brainstorming session, it works best with between four and 10 participants. The group begins by selecting a scribe who write the problem on the flipchart and will then go around the group in turn, asking each member to suggest one solution which is then written on the flipchart. All ideas are recorded, no matter how silly or way out they appear. Colour is used and ideas are written randomly and haphazardly on the paper (not in a linear fashion!). Team members are encouraged to participate as much as possible during the round-robin (usually two rounds of the groups) and as members fail to come up with new ideas, the leader should switch to popcorn mode where people chip in with ideas at random. Quite often the best ideas will evolve during the popcorn session as people have warmed up to the process and are beginning to build on previous suggestions. Once everyone has begun to dry up, the brainstorming session is over and the ideas are sorted. During the sorting, similar ideas are considered and some ideas will be eliminated – so long as everyone in the group agrees. When there is a final selection of ideas, a decision making tool may be used to identify which top solutions will be taken forward for further investigation and analysis.

During this phase a decision making tool like the 5-point scoring system is useful. This is particularly good in groups or teams as everyone will have a voice and a part in the decision making process. Each team member has a total of five points to allocate to the options and they decide how they want to split these. Some may opt to put all five points on one option, others may split it between two, three or even four options. Depending on the size of the group, either each person will write their scores against their option or the scribe will go around the group and write up points against each option. Once everyone has given their points, the end scores are totalled for each option to find out the top potential solutions. There will usually be two or three options which will be taken forward for further analysis.

Learning Bite:

Taking the problem from earlier, either on your own or with a small group, come up with some different alternatives for resolving the problem. Once you have a number of options, narrow them down to just two or three.

Analysis of Solutions

There are various ways that solutions may be analysed or evaluated. These include:

Advantages vs disadvantages – considering the pros and cons for each of the solutions. This can work well if red is used for disadvantages and green is used for advantages as it makes it visually easier to identify if a solution is likely to be successful or if the cons outweigh the pros.

Ranking – looking at solutions against certain criteria which may include timeframes, available budgets or resources and ranking each solution accordingly on a scale of 1 to 5 where 1 is low and 5 is high. Solutions with the lowest ratings are therefore likely to be less risky and have a better chance of success.

De Bono's Six Thinking Hats - Edward de Bono has been called the master of creative thinking. He developed the concept of the Six Thinking Hats to encourage creativity in problem solving. The objective is to look at a problem from different perspectives. It can be used in two ways: to work through the problem systematically wearing a different hat in turn, or to allocate a hat to each person within the group or team who then gives their view of the solution from that viewpoint. The six hats are:

- The **White Hat (or Chef's Hat)** – this suggests paper and concerns information. When we wear the white hat we are gathering data, facts and figures. We ask questions concerning the information we have and need, including the type of data required, the format, how often we may need the information, where we may find the information and who can help us.

- The **Green Hat (or Baseball Cap)** – this colour suggests vegetation and organic growth which encourages life and energy. This is the creative hat for putting forward new ideas and brainstorming suggestions without a logical base. It is used for proposing new ideas and alternatives, for lateral thinking and for suggesting modifications and variations for an idea. Brainstorming activities are conducted with the green hat.

- The **Black Hat (or Judge's Hat)** – this is usually the most useful hat as it focuses on the potential disadvantages of the solutions. It is used with caution and with logic to point out possible problems based on facts. It uses past experience, points out the risks and potential failures and prevents us from doing anything that may be harmful. However, over-use can be dangerous.

- The **Yellow Hat (or Sombrero)** – as the colour suggests sunshine, the yellow hat is full of optimism and points out advantages and benefits. With the yellow hat we make a real effort to find the value in proposals and to seek out the good points, even if we do not like the suggestion itself. It is logical and positive.

- The **Red Hat (or Christmas Hat)** – this suggest fire and warmth. The red hat concerns emotions, feelings, intuition and personal values. With the red hat, you have the opportunity to put forward feelings without any explanation. Your emotions exist and the red hat gives you permission to put these feelings forward. This is a hat that is frequently forgotten in analysis of potential solutions as these are factors that are considered less crucial in times of profit and growth. However, it is important to remember that people are affected by problems and solutions and to understand the impact this may have which may then affect motivation and in turn productivity.

- The **Blue Hat (or Policeman's Helmet)** – this is the hat for the facilitator to wear or the person who is managing the process to ensure that everyone is involved and aware of the process and the problem under discussion. The blue hat needs to be used at the beginning of the session in order to define what we are discussing, to look at the thinking process, keeping track and summarising. This includes looking at how the solution fits with current practice, policies and procedures.

-

Learning Bite:

Taking your top two solutions, work through De Bono's Six Thinking Hats to analyse your solutions. Which is now the better solution to implement?

Decision and Planning

Whichever tool is used to analyse and evaluate, you will usually find that one solution comes out higher than the others and this is the one which will be taken forward, whilst the others may be parked for later consideration if required. The decision making is therefore made much easier with good analysis.

Now a solution has been decided on, the planning part of the process begins. This involves pulling together a list of activities required, allocating roles and responsibilities to other people in the team and deciding on a timeframe.

The first step is to begin with a list of activities and resources required. You may also want to think about how long each task is going to take and who will be responsible. You may want to use a pro-forma like the one below

	Activity	Resource Required	Responsible Person	Time Required
1				
2				
3				

Once you have confirmed your activity list, you will want to schedule the activities. The most suitable tool for this is a Gantt chart which provides a visual timeline of tasks and deadlines for each activity. More information is available in the chapter on Business Tools.

Learning Bite:

How are you going to implement your proposed solution? Draw up an activity list and a Gantt chart to show the timeframe

Implementation of solution

When the planning has been properly carried out, the implementation of a solution will usually be straightforward. Remember to communicate with everyone who is involved or who may be impacted. Consider any implications that may arise from the implementation and find ways to manage them to minimize disruption.

Take the following problem as an example:

A call centre has received a higher than usual level of complaints. The root cause analysis has identified that lack of organisational knowledge is resulting in call centre operators routing calls wrongly. The preferred solution is identified as provision of training for all operators to help them understand the organisation structure and workings better. The short-term impact of this solution will be an increased number of complaints due to short staffing whilst operators are taken away from the workplace for training. As this is a short-term impact and the solution should result in increased customer satisfaction and lower level of complaints in the medium term, it is considered a viable solution.

Review

Whilst we normally follow the first seven steps of problem solving successfully, we fail to complete the cycle by reviewing the effectiveness of the solution. This may be due to a number of reasons including workload, time and other pressures. However, reviewing a solution is important in identifying whether the problem has been resolved, if the fix is fit for purpose and if there have been any associated problems occurring as a result. Depending on the initial problem and solution, it is best to review after one month and again after six months as this gives a better picture of effectiveness. This does not need to be a time-consuming process and should involve a simple review with those concerned.

Another valid reason for reviewing the effectiveness of a solution is to look at the problem solving process itself. Consider what was done well, what could have been done better and was the analysis of potential solutions valid given the benefit of hindsight. Questions like these encourage reflection and will help you to develop your problem solving abilities.

Learning Bite:

How will you review the implementation of your solution? What questions might you ask to ascertain if it has resolved the initial problem?

Managing Change

As we have already looked at understanding change and managing its impact on people in the previous section on People Management, we will focus here on the tools used in planning and managing change.

Change management programmes are an important part of a manager's role and learning the appropriate tools and techniques will help you to become more effective in planning and managing change of all sorts. Change management is akin to project management and involves many of the same tools.

In the previous chapter we looked at the problem solving process and generating and implementing solutions. Often these will involve a change management programme, so let's begin by looking at what the term 'change management' actually means. There are many definitions and one of the best is provided by the BNET Business Dictionary as 'the coordination of a structured period of transition from situation A to situation B in order to achieve lasting change within an organisation'. Successful change management is therefore moving from one stage to another and taking the people with you.

Planning the change management is the most important part of the process and the following provides the steps involved:

- **Step one** - Agree terms of reference for change

- **Step two** - Plan the change - time, team, activities, resources, financials

- **Step three** - Communicate the change and plan to project team

- **Step four** - Agree and delegate actions. Motivate, inform, encourage staff to enable the change

- **Step five** - Check, measure, review project progress; adjust plans, keep communicating as appropriate

- **Step six** - Complete change and review

We will look at each of these steps in detail and consider the tools which are helpful at each stage.

Step One – Terms of Reference (TORs)

The terms of reference provide the information you need to plan the change. These will typically cover:

- **Purpose of change** - including an overview of the change and required outputs.

- **Objectives** of the change – these should be SMART and concise.

- **Scope** – the boundaries of the change – this may refer to the departments / people involved or may refer to the depth of the change. Identify key areas within and without the boundaries.

- **Timeframe** – deadlines for implementation, review and any milestones identified.

- **Responsibilities** – who will be responsible for different tasks within the change with level of responsibility and accountability.

- **Resources** – this may refer to the people involved in the change, the equipment or the material available or other resources including advice and information. You will want a summary of all resources available.

- **Budget** – if there are costs involved in implementing the change.

Once you have clarified the terms of reference you have a clear way forward to plan the implementation.

This is arguably the most important part of change: 'Failing to plan is planning to fail'. Working with the TORs, you can consider the implementation plan. For this you will want to use the following tools:

- **Stakeholder analysis** – more details available in the next chapter. This looks at anyone who has an interest in the change and their level of interest and involvement, and will be used to inform your communication plan.

- **Communication plan** – working with the stakeholder analysis you can prepare a communication plan. Kipling's Men are a useful tool in considering the appropriate level of communication – who, what, where, when, why and how. You may find it useful to use a template like the one below:

Who?	What?	When?	How?
Who are the people you are going to communicate with? These will be your stakeholders and you may want to name as individuals or as groups. List their names in the column below.	What level of information do they need? What sort of information will they be interested in? Rate this as high level, medium level, low level.	Consider the timing. When will you communicate with them? Will this be a regular (ie weekly or monthly) or one-off communication? This may be influenced by the level of information required.	What media will you use? Consider the best media – email, written, telephone, face-to-face for each stakeholder / group.

- **Activity list** – this lists all the activities involved in planning the change. You can make it as high or low level as you want to, although the more detailed ensures that there is less scope for overlooking key activities. You may want to refer to the activity list in the previous chapter for this purpose.

- **Schedule** – there are different tools you can use here to schedule the activities, list responsibilities and identify key dates. The most popular one is a Gantt chart as it is quite simple and provides a visual tool. It is a good idea to make a large version of this and display in the department so people feel involved and can monitor progress of the change. Other tools you may consider are PERT and Critical Path Analysis. There are more details of all these tools in the next chapter together with examples.

- **Budget** – if a budget is required, you will need to identify financial considerations. This will include the expenditure and any return on investment. In some organisations you may need to complete a business plan which will require approval.

Step Three – Communicate

Now that you have the project plan in place, you are ready to communicate. You will have probably already done some communication in the planning stage; however, this is the time to formally communicate the change and the implementation plan.

Ideally this will be done in a meeting with everyone involved in the change. This should be led by the manager implementing the change and should include the following:

- Purpose and objectives of the change

- Benefits of change

- Timeframe and implementation plan

- How people will be affected

- How people will be involved – or to invite involvement from team

Remember that staff may be feeling negative towards the change and a positive attitude here is essential. Allow plenty of time for questions and answer as honestly as possible providing as much information as appropriate.

Step four - Agree and Delegate Actions

Agree with staff involved who will be doing what, consider the timeframe and remember to delegate responsibility / accountability where appropriate.

Involve people as much as possible to avoid them feeling that change is being done to them. This will require you to motivate staff and empower them, encouraging them to enable the change.

Provide as much information as you can (without overloading people) to empower staff to implement the change.

Ensure everyone has a copy of the implementation plan and Gantt chart (or schedule) so they can monitor progress.

Step Five – Review and Monitor Progress

As the implementation proceeds, review on a regular basis. Depending on the change and your schedule this may be on a daily, weekly or monthly basis. Ask people to give progress reports so that you can keep track of what is happening. Where there are slippages, remember to adjust the plan accordingly.

Keep communicating with those involve to ensure change is implemented and people are involved.

Step Six – Complete Change

This is an important step and is frequently forgotten! Once the change has been implemented, thank everyone involved. Give people feedback where they have been involved.

Review the change – has it been successful? And consider how you have managed the change. Think about what went well, what didn't go so well and what you would change for another time. Go back to your business tools and consider how well they applied – ask yourself the following questions:

- Did you stick to the timeframes in your schedule?

- Did you achieve your objectives?

- Were the resource requirements appropriate?

- How effective was your communication plan?

- Was your stakeholder analysis appropriate? Did you need to change it as you progressed the change?

- How detailed was your activity list? Were there actions missing?

- How did you manage your team through the change?

Learning Bite:

Consider a recent change which you have either managed or been involved in implementing. Think about the questions above and identify ways in which you would approach the next change.

How you plan change will be influenced by your own individual style as a manager given the situation. There are four different styles of planning and implementing change:

- **Collaborative** – this approach means involve the people who are affected by the change, working with them and empowering them so that they feel they are creating the change rather than have the change 'done' to them. This includes gaining their commitment and encouraging them to invest in the change. Whilst this is probably one of the preferred ways of planning and managing change, it is also the most time-consuming and can be a barrier given the pressures of most organisations.

- **Consultative** - this offers an alternative to collaboration as it provides a compromise showing that the manager is listening to people's concerns and taking them into account. A consultative approach offers a balance between collaboration and pushing people into change through coercion.

- **Directive** – whilst there may still be a high level of communication between manager and staff it is mainly one-way with the manager communicating to the staff without really listening or taking account of their concerns. This works on the principle of pushing people into change and driving the change through. For this style to be effective, the manager needs to offer a lot of support and a high level of communication.

- **Coercive** – this style is driving change through with very little attention given to the staff, their thoughts, feelings or needs. These changes are implemented in a directive, forceful way which will cause shock to the staff involved and may result in demotivated or rebellious staff.

Each style has its uses and its benefits but depends very much on the manager and the situation.

John Kotter's Change Management Model

Whilst there are a numerous models and templates for managing change, John Kotter's eight-stage model remains one of the most popular. This is explored in the simple tale of a penguin colony facing change in 'Our Iceberg is Melting'[xlvi].

The eight stages, condensed, are:

Stage One – Establish a Sense of Urgency — encourage people to think, "let's go, we need to change things". People need deadlines to motivate and inspire. Begin to consider potential crises and establish timeframes.

Stage Two – Create the Guiding Team — this involves putting together the team that will implement the change. They need to have the right level of power to lead the change and motivate staff and the influence to get the group working together like a team. Quite often a team may have a sponsor or someone in a senior position who will use their power to influence others although their role in the working team may be much smaller.

Stage Three – Develop the Vision and a Strategy — the "Guiding Team" create the right vision and strategy to help direct the change effort. Typically the vision will precede the change. However, now the team are on-board they need to develop the vision further, flesh out the activities and decide on a strategy for implementation.

Stage Four – Communicate the Change Vision — use every vehicle possible to constantly communicate the new vision and strategies. People start to buy into the vision and this is reflected in their behaviour.

Stage Five - Empower Broad-Based Action — this stage focuses on getting rid of obstacles and barriers which may include changing systems or structures so that everyone feels able to act on the vision. Encourage staff to take risks and embrace new ideas, activities and actions.

Stage Six - Generate Short Term Wins — making things happen quickly so that people see the benefit of change will motivate people to take action. Visible performance improvements and benefits will encourage staff.

Stage Seven - Don't Let Up — keep the changes happening until the vision is fulfilled. This may include recruiting, promoting and developing people who can implement the change. Reinvigorate the process with new projects, themes, and change agents.

Stage Eight - Change Stick — involves embedding the change and making new practices feel like standard without reverting to traditional methods. Kotter believes in creating better performance through customer- and productivity-orientated behaviour, better leadership and more effective management. This stage involves forgetting what used to be and the way things were done and embracing the new ways of working to embed the change and move to the new level.

Business Tools

Whilst there is a plethora of business tools around to help you in managing projects, tasks and workloads, the following are the most commonly used and provide an introduction into using different business models and tools.

The ones we will look at here include:

- SWOT analysis

- PEST or PESTLE analysis

- Ishikawa (Fishbone) diagram

- Gantt chart

- Critical Path analysis

- PERT

- Stakeholder analysis

- Force Field analysis

SWOT Analysis

A SWOT analysis is a snapshot of a business or situation at a given time. It is typically only valid for a short period of time, depending on the type of SWOT and the purpose for its use. To prepare a SWOT analysis you would begin by identifying the relevant situation, purpose or objective of the project or business. This will then be used to determine the Strengths, Weaknesses, Opportunities and Threats.

Strengths are the internal assets, strong points or positive characteristics of the situation. These are usually seen as an advantage over competitors or forces in favour. These may include reputation, competitive edge, pricing, resources available, facilities, workforce expertise and experience, customer base, product / service range and organisation size.

Weaknesses are the vulnerable points, known as issues or flaws, which expose the organisation and will be seen as a disadvantage in relation to other companies. These can be seen as similar to the strengths in terms of deficits or shortages in these areas.

Opportunities are external to the organisation which may provide the openings or breaks to improve a situation, increase effectiveness, grow profits or business and explore new markets. These may include current market place position, niche markets, identified new markets, changing needs resulting from the economy, environment, demographics and legislation.

Threats are also external to the organisation and identify the problems that will hinder the project or business, create greater risks and may prevent success. These could include competition from other organisations, changes in legislation, economy, environment and emerging organisations.

Conducting a SWOT analysis can be an illuminating activity that helps to expose opportunities for improvement and development. It will also help in deciding whether the initial objective is viable, whether it needs modification or whether a new objective is required.

Whilst it is a useful tool in evaluating and analysing business opportunities, it also has benefits as a method used in various other situations for example in promoting recommendations, identifying personal development needs and decision making.

Please see figure 23 below for a template for a SWOT analysis:

Strengths	Weaknesses
- Internal	- Internal
- Helpful	- Harmful

Opportunities	Threats
- External	- External
- Helpful	- Harmful

Learning Point:

Consider your team / department and do a SWOT analysis.
Where can you see scope for developing?

PEST or PESTLE Analysis

This is another strategic analysing tool which is particularly useful in identifying new opportunities for products or services, evaluating the business position and looking at future direction taking account of macro-environmental factors. Initially known as a PEST, some people have added an additional one or two elements, so it has become known as PESTLE.

Political – this considers the influence of a government on the business particularly in areas of tax, funding, trade restrictions and political stability. It may also include preferred services that governments may need providing or equally services that are not required.

Economic – this is the current state of the economy including taxes, interest rates, inflation rates, foreign exchange tariffs, recessions and rates of growth. This will impact on the growth and expansion of businesses particularly those operating in an international environment.

Social - this considers social trends, demographics (growth rate, birth rate, age distribution), attitudes towards careers and job market. Legislation changes regarding retirement ages will influence recruitment policies. Organisations may adapt management strategies according to social trends and changing demands.

Technological – this considers the advances in technology and the changes this brings. It will determine routes to market, production levels, costs, pricing and quality. Technology will also influence areas like research and development, customer service and marketing.

Legal – this takes accounts of required legislation that may impact on the business. This will include employment law, health and safety legislation, discrimination laws, European working time directives. Legislation may affect the running of a business, the operating costs and the demand for products and services.

Environmental – this includes the influence of environmental and ecological changes including climate, pandemics, trends, tourism and weather. This will also cover environmental responsibility in terms of recycling and pollution. These factors influence how companies operate and may create new opportunities.

Variations on this classic PESTLE analysis include:

- LONGPESTLE – Local, National and Global which will service to contextualise multi-national organisations

- STEER - Socio-cultural, Technological, Economic, Ecological and Regulatory factors

- SLEPT – Social, Legal, Economic, Political and Technological (simple rearrangement of elements)

Learning Point:

Consider your team / department and do a PEST / PESTLE analysis. Compare it with the SWOT analysis you have done and look at the different areas.

Ishikawa (Fishbone diagram)

Ishikawa[xlvii] diagrams, better known as fishbone diagrams, were developed by quality expert, Kaoru Ishikawa in the 1960s. They are causal diagrams intended to prevent quality defects. They are a useful tool in root cause analysis as a fishbone diagram provides a framework to consider different factors. They take the shape of a fishbone with the different categories coming off the main backbone and notes made around each of these headings.

Causes are usually categorised into main headings – although the number and headings themselves will vary according to industry requirements. A general fishbone will typically include the following:

People – anyone who is involved in the process. Ask what skills are needed? What skills do people have? Are they aware and trained? What is the impact on people? What level of experience is available / required?

Methods – what methods have been used? What processes are in place? Are these processes working? Are there specific policies? Do you need a policy? What about legislation and regulation?

Equipment – this will include machinery, tools and information technology. What is required to complete the job? Is the equipment sufficient? Are upgrades needed? Is the equipment being properly used? Is equipment properly maintained?

Materials – any materials required to perform the task. This may include raw materials, machine parts or office stationery. Is all material available? Is the material quality sufficient? Are there newer materials available which may be more effective?

Measurements – what measurements are in place? How is data recorded and reported? What measurements are taken to ensure quality? Are targets / goals the same for everyone? Are people aware of the objectives and measurements?

Environment – is the environment appropriate? Are the working conditions satisfactory? Is any special environment required? Are noise levels comfortable for people working? Are staff given sufficient breaks?

Analysis of a completed Ishikawa will usually provide the root cause(s) for problems or defects.

Different industries have different headings. For example, manufacturing companies and service companies use the following:

Manufacturing Industry– 6Ms	Service Industry – 4Ps
Machines	Policies
Methods	Procedures
Materials	People
Measurements	Plant / technology
Mother Nature (environment)	
Manpower (people)	

Gantt Chart

Gantt charts were developed by Henry Lawrence Gantt around 1910 with the purpose of providing a visual tool for showing the different phases of a project. They are widely used in project management and are useful for many different purposes. These include the construction of the Hoover Dam and the planning of the US interstate highway system. A Gantt chart is a horizontal bar chart where the length of the line or bar represents the length of the task, allowing you to assess how long a task should take, determine the resources required and identify the order in which tasks should be carried out.

Activities need to be identified as 'sequential' or 'parallel'. Sequential tasks are dependent activities which need to be completed in a sequence with each stage completed (more or less) before the next stage can begin. Parallel tasks are not dependent and can therefore be carried out independently of other tasks.

To prepare a Gantt chart:

List all activities required and for each identify if it is parallel or sequential. If sequential, identify the activities on which they are dependent. For each task, estimate the length of time required for completion.

The next stage involves the plotting of the Gantt chart. This can be done on Word (using a table), Excel (easiest) or specialist project software, for example Microsoft Project. Begin by identifying the start date and completion date.

The Gantt chart is a matrix with a horizontal axis representing the total timeline for the project. This will be broken down into increments depending on the length of the project, for example days, weeks or months.

The vertical axis represents the tasks that make up the project and the first column will be the list of tasks (numbered) required. The second column may include who is responsible for this task, although this information is not always included.

The Gantt chart will then be completed by drawing the horizontal lines task by task, the length of each determined by the length of the task, the start date being determined by the nature of the task. Some Gantt charts show the start and end dates on the line. Others do not. Milestones may be plotted on a Gantt chart to indicate review dates, meetings or other significant events. These are shown as a diamond shape on the appropriate line.

The following table shows you a simple Gantt chart with a short list of numbered tasks. This does not show the list of activities for the numbers, but offers a simple chart for demonstration purposes. From this example we can see that task 1 is parallel and will take the duration of the project, task 2 is also parallel and will take most of the time. Tasks 3, 4, 5 and 6 are sequential and are dependent on each of the previous tasks being completed.

Task	Who	Year					
		Jan	Feb	Mar	April	May	Jun
1							
2							
3							
4							
5							
6							
7							

Critical Path Analysis

A Critical Path Analysis is another scheduling tool used for plotting timeframes. Also known as Critical Path Method (CPM), it was developed in the 1950s and is successfully used in many planning tasks for example construction, software development, research and other development projects. Similar to Gantt, you begin by establishing the list of tasks, planned length of each activity and the dependencies of the tasks. Using this information you can calculate the longest time required to complete the project – this is known as the critical path.

This is then plotted with each activity shown in a circle and connected to other circles (tasks) using arrows. Conventionally these run from left to right. The length of time required for the task is written above the arrow and the task itself is written below the arrow.

In the example below, the first two tasks – interviews and survey – are parallel tasks and can be completed at the same time. Both will take one week and need to be completed before the analysis can begin.

In CPA the activities are referred to as the numbers in the circles. For example, interviews would be 3 to 4, survey would be 1 to 2 and action plan would be 5 to 6.

Activities are not drawn to scale (unlike a Gantt) and each arrow will be the same length regardless of length of time required. The numbers in the upper quadrant of each circle will show the earliest start time for the task. CPA conventionally starts at 0 so in the example below, interviews will start at 0 and analysis will start at 1, with the units for this example being in weeks.

From the simple example below in figure 24, we can see that the critical path required for completion would be four weeks.

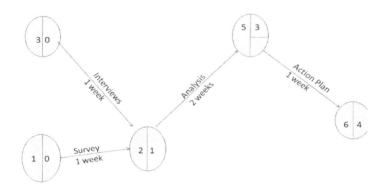

PERT

PERT is a variation on Critical Path Analysis, with the exception that it uses a different formula for calculating the time available for each task. It considers the shortest time available to complete the task and the longest time available and then uses the following formula to produce a timeframe for each task:

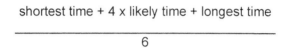

$$\frac{\text{shortest time} + 4 \text{ x likely time} + \text{longest time}}{6}$$

It is then plotted in the same way as a critical path analysis with nodes linked by arrows.

All of these scheduling tools serve a purpose. However, it is best to select the tool which you feel most comfortable using and maintaining. Once you have a draft schedule, consider how to make it more realistic. Look for any errors or mistakes, consider the estimated timeframes and look for oversights or omissions of tasks. Identify if all activities have been planned for and allocation of tasks to individuals in terms of timeframe.

Stakeholder Analysis

A stakeholder analysis is a powerful tool in the planning of projects and in managing change to identify the key stakeholders together with their level of interest and influence. This analysis then informs communication and activities required.

A stakeholder is anyone who has an interest in the business. This will include all staff, customers, suppliers, third parties involved in the business, providers, local community, shareholders and others depending on the business.

The first step is to identify all stakeholders.

The second step is to place them on your stakeholder grid. Stakeholders will fall into four categories:

High interest–high influence: these are the people you need to actively involve and keep close.

High interest-low influence: these people have a high interest but little influence in decision making; however, they need to be kept informed. Quite often these will be staff involved in the change or project.

Low interest-high influence: these are potentially quite powerful people. Whilst their level of interest may not be high, they need to be informed (usually at a broader level) to ensure they are aware of what is going on as they have influence over the project.

Low interest-low influence: these are your lowest concern; however, they need to be monitored.

The third step is to plan communications and information according to their level of power and interest.

An example of a stakeholder analysis can be seen in the following diagram in figure 25:

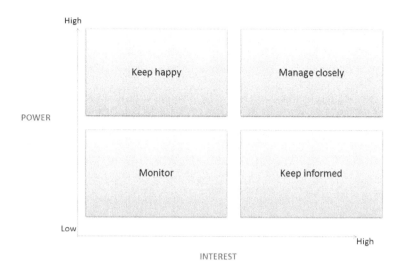

Learning Point:

Thinking about your team and the service you provide, identify your stakeholders and plot them on a stakeholder analysis. How may this affect the way you communicate with people?

Force Field Analysis

Developed by Kurt Lewin during the 1940s, force field analysis is a powerful tool for identifying the forces that influence a situation. These may be positive (forces for) or negative (forces against) and which will impact on any decision to be taken.

It may be used for different purposes including decision making and selling a solution. To complete a force field analysis begin by putting the problem or situation in a centre box. The forces for are then identified on the left hand side of the box and the forces against on the right hand side. A simple version will only show the forces, a more useful version will be weighted. To do this, score each force for and against on a scale of 1 to 5 where 1 is weak and 5 is strong.

A force field analysis is typically drawn showing arrows, the length of which depends on the weight (or score) of the force.

If you are using this as a decision making tool, you can add the scores for forces for and similarly for forces against to find out the best way forward. If you are using it to sell a solution, you may want to consider the barriers that the other person / party may put forward and identify possible solutions or returns on investment that will sway the decision in your favour and positively influence the outcome.

Figure 26 below shows an example of a simple force field analysis where the arrows show the different weights. From this you can determine that the forces for outweigh the forces against.

Conclusion

This book has covered some of the core responsibilities of management. However, it doesn't cover every aspect nor does it provide solutions to the problems you may find in your role.

The further you progress in your role as a manager, the more you will learn. Consider keeping a reflective learning journal to write down your thoughts and learning points.

If you have completed all the learning bites and various assessments throughout this book, you will have definitely increased your own self-awareness. The key to successfully managing others is first to know yourself and second to manage yourself. You will then be an effective role model and your tasks as a manager will be much easier.

And good luck in your role!

About the Author

Desiree Cox is a professional and management development consultant with eighteen years' experience. Passionate about helping people to develop their full potential, she enjoys the challenge of working with teams and individuals of all levels.

Her training company, Praeceptor Consulting, was founded in 2002 and offers training, workshops, assessments centres, coaching and development for staff of all levels in both private and public sectors. As an accredited centre for the Institute of Leadership and Management qualifications, Praeceptor Consulting provides training for delegates in all aspects of leadership and management.

Desiree has a degree in Psychology and Management together with Diplomas in NLP, Performance Coaching, Writing, IT training, Teaching and Management. She has had several articles published in magazines together with regular business book reviews. Her first book, "An Introduction to Office Management for Secretaries" (Cassell), was published in 1998.

If you would like to keep up to date with management or simply to get in touch, please visit www.thehungrymanager.co.uk

References

[i] www.businessdictionary.com accessed 12/1/2012

[ii] www.businessdictionary.com accessed 12/1/2012

[iii] Fayol, Henri (1917) (in French), Administration industrielle et générale; prévoyance, organisation, commandement, coordination, controle, Paris, H. Dunod et E. Pinat
[iv] Henry A. Landsberger, *Hawthorne Revisited*, Ithaca, 1958

[v] Kotter, John P. (1988). The Leadership Factor

[vi] Arvey, R. D., Rotundo, M., Johnson, W., Zhang, Z., & McGue, M. (2006). The determinants of leadership role occupancy: Genetic and personality factors. Leadership Quarterly, 17, 1-20

[vii] Hersey, P. and Blanchard, K. H. (1977). Management of Organizational Behavior 3rd Edition– Utilizing Human Resources. New Jersey/Prentice Hall

[viii] Hersey, P. (1985). The situational leader. New York, NY: Warner Books

[ix] Blanchard, Kenneth H., Patricia Zigarmi, and Drea Zigarmi. Leadership and the One Minute Manager: Increasing Effectiveness through Situational Leadership. New York: Morrow, 1985. Print

[x] Tannenbaum, A.S. and Schmitt, W.H. (1958). "How to choose a leadership pattern". Harvard Business Review, 36, March-April, 95-101

[xi] Adair, J.E. (1973), "Action-Centred Leadership". McGraw-Hill, London

[xii] McGregor, D (1960), "The Human Side of Enterprise", McGraw-Hill

[xiii] Survey conducted by Praeceptor Consulting, January 2012

[xiv] Luft, J.; Ingham, H. (1950). "The Johari window, a graphic model of interpersonal awareness". Proceedings of the western training laboratory in group development (Los Angeles: UCLA)

[xv] Handy, Charles (2000). 21 Ideas for Managers. San Francisco: Jossey-Bass

[xvi] Gibbs G. Learning by Doing: A Guide to Teaching and Learning Methods [monograph online]. Reproduced by the Geography Discipline Network; 2001

[xvii] Mehrabian, A. (1971). *Silent messages*, Wadsworth, California: Belmont

[xviii] Cox, D (1998). Introduction to Office Management for Secretaries, Cassell, London

[xix] Mehrabian, A. (1971). *Silent messages*, Wadsworth, California: Belmont

[xx] Drucker, Peter F., "The Practice of Management", 1954

[xxi] http://www.goodreads.com/quotes/show/124454 accessed 8/3/2012

[xxii] Goleman, Daniel. (1998). *Working with Emotional Intelligence,* Bloomsbury

[xxiii] Honey,P (1994). *101 ways to develop your people, without really trying!* Peter Honey Publications, Berkshire

[xxiv] http://www.hse.gov.uk/stress/furtheradvice/whatisstress.htm accessed 15/4/2012

[xxv] Truss, Soane, Edwards, Wisom, Croll and Burnett (2006*). "Working Life: Employee Attitudes and Engagement 2006",* CIPD Enterprises Ltd

[xxvi] Covey, Stephen (1989), *"7 Habits of Highly Effective People",* Simon & Schuster Ltd

[xxvii] Archer, Dr Simon (2003), "*Sleep*", Volume 26, Issue 04

[xxviii] Katzenbach, J.R. & Smith, D.K. (1993), *The Wisdom of Teams: Creating the High-performance Organization* Boston: Harvard Business School

[xxix] Janis, IL (1982), *Victims of Group Think: A Psychological Study of Foreign Policy Decisions and Fiascos* (2nd edn), Boston, MA, Houghton Mifflin

[xxx] Tuckman, Bruce (1965). *"Developmental sequence in small groups"*, Psychological Bulletin **63** (6): 384–99

[xxxi] Belbin, M (1981), *Management Teams – Why They succeed or fail,* Butterworth Heinemann Ltd

[xxxii] Honey, P. & Mumford, A. (2000). *The learning styles helper's guide.* Maidenhead: Peter Honey Publications Ltd.

[xxxiii] Anderson, L W, & Krathwohl D R (eds.) (2001). *A Taxonomy for Learning, Teaching, and Assessing: A Revision of Bloom's Taxonomy of Educational Objectives.* New York: Longman

[xxxiv] http://dictionary.cambridge.org/dictionary/british accessed 10/10/2012

[xxxv] http://psychology.about.com/od/mindex/g/motivation-definition.htm accessed 8/10/2012

[xxxvi] Herzberg, F., Mausner, B. & Snyderman, B.B. 1959, *The Motivation to Work.* John Wiley. New York.

[xxxvii] McClelland, David C., The Achieving Society (1961). University of Illinois at Urbana-Champaign's Academy for Entrepreneurial Leadership Historical Research Reference in Entrepreneurship

[xxxviii]

http://oxforddictionaries.com/definition/english/communication accessed 16/10/2012 xxxix Boddy, D. and Buchanan, D. (1992) *Take the Lead: Interpersonal Skills for Project Managers*, London, Prentice Hall

xl Mehrabian, Albert (1971). *Silent Messages* (1st ed.). Belmont, CA: Wadsworth. ISBN 0-534-00910-7.

xli Morris, Desmond (1967), *The Naked Ape: A Zoologist's Study of the Human Animal*, reprinted 1999, Delta

xlii http://oxforddictionaries.com/definition/english/change - accessed 19/10/ 2012

xliii Oakley P, Greaves E. Restructuring. From command to demand-cultural consequences. *Health Service J* 1995; 105: 32-33

xliv Schein E (2010), Organizational Culture and Leadership, John Wiley & Sons

xlv Handy, Charles B. (1976) *Understanding Organizations,* Oxford University Press

xlvi Kotter John P, Rathgeber, H (2006), Our Iceberge is Melting, Macmillan

xlvii Ishikawa, Kaoru, (1968). Guide to Quality Control (Japanese), JUSE Press, Ltd., Tokyo

Printed in Great Britain
by Amazon

59841711R00132